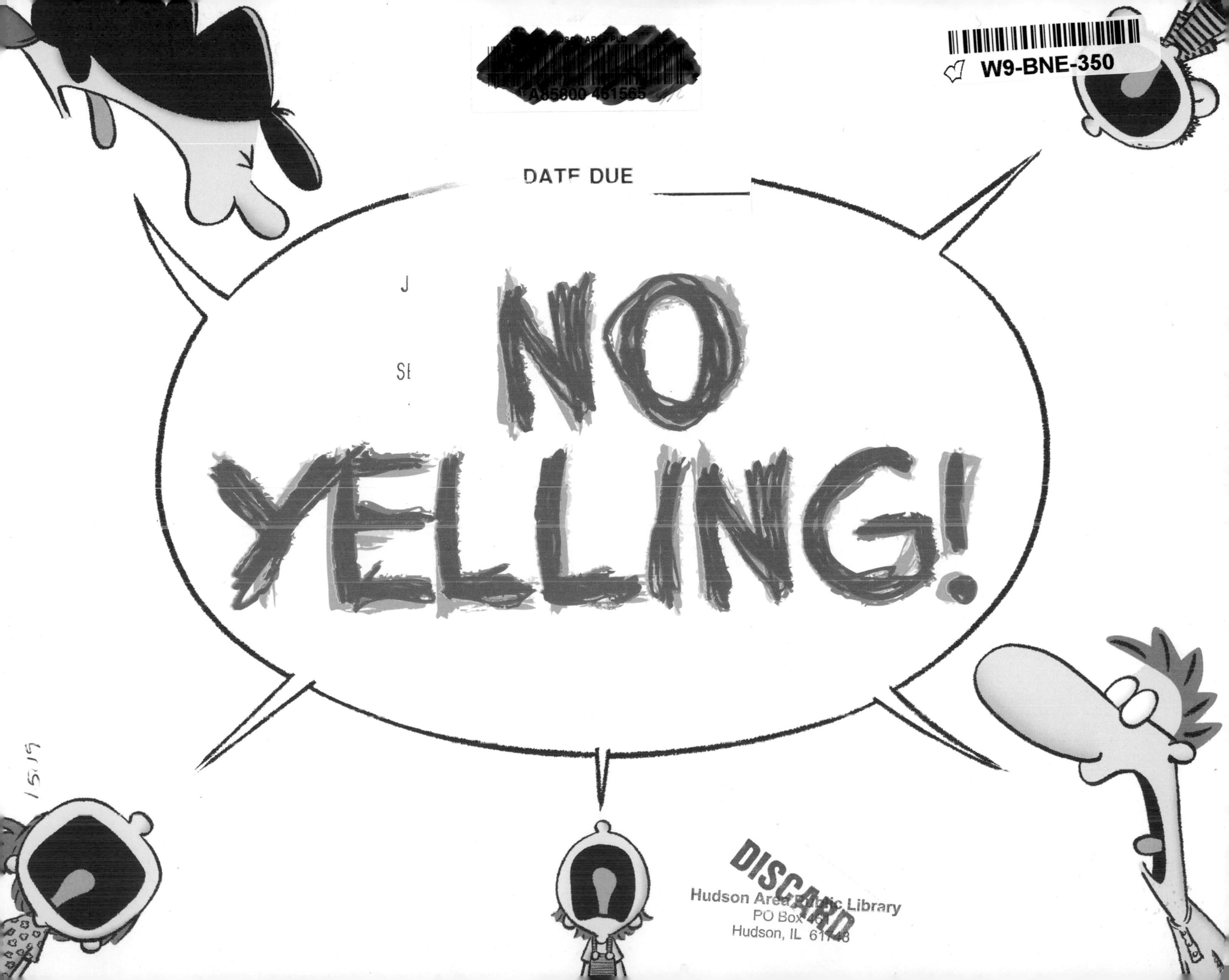
NO YELLING!

Other Baby Blues® Books from Andrews McMeel Publishing

Guess Who Didn't Take a Nap?
I Thought Labor Ended When the Baby Was Born
We Are Experiencing Parental Difficulties . . . Please Stand By
Night of the Living Dad
I Saw Elvis in My Ultrasound
One More and We're Outnumbered!
Check, Please . . .
threats, bribes & videotape
If I'm a Stay-at-Home Mom, Why Am I Always in the Car?
Lift and Separate
I Shouldn't Have to Scream More Than Once!
Motherhood Is Not for Wimps
Baby Blues®: Unplugged
Dad to the Bone
Never a Dry Moment
Two Plus One Is Enough
Playdate: Category 5
Our Server Is Down
Something Chocolate This Way Comes
Briefcase Full of Baby Blues®
Night Shift
The Day Phonics Kicked In
My Space
The Natural Disorder of Things
We Were Here First
Ambushed! In the Family Room
Cut!
Eat, Cry, Poop
Scribbles at an Exhibition
Bedlam
Wetter, Louder, Stickier

Treasuries

The Super-Absorbent Biodegradable Family-Size Baby Blues®
Baby Blues®: Ten Years and Still in Diapers
Butt-Naked Baby Blues®
Wall-to-Wall Baby Blues®
Driving Under the Influence of Children
Framed!
X-Treme Parenting
BBXX: Baby Blues: Decades 1 and 2

Gift Book

It's a Boy
It's a Girl

NO YELLING!

rick kirkman
jerry scott

Scrapbook

No. 32

Andrews McMeel
Publishing®

Kansas City · Sydney · London

To my dad and role model,
Donald Scott
1927—2014

—J.S.

To my biggest fan,
Worth Kirkman
1930—2015

—R.K.

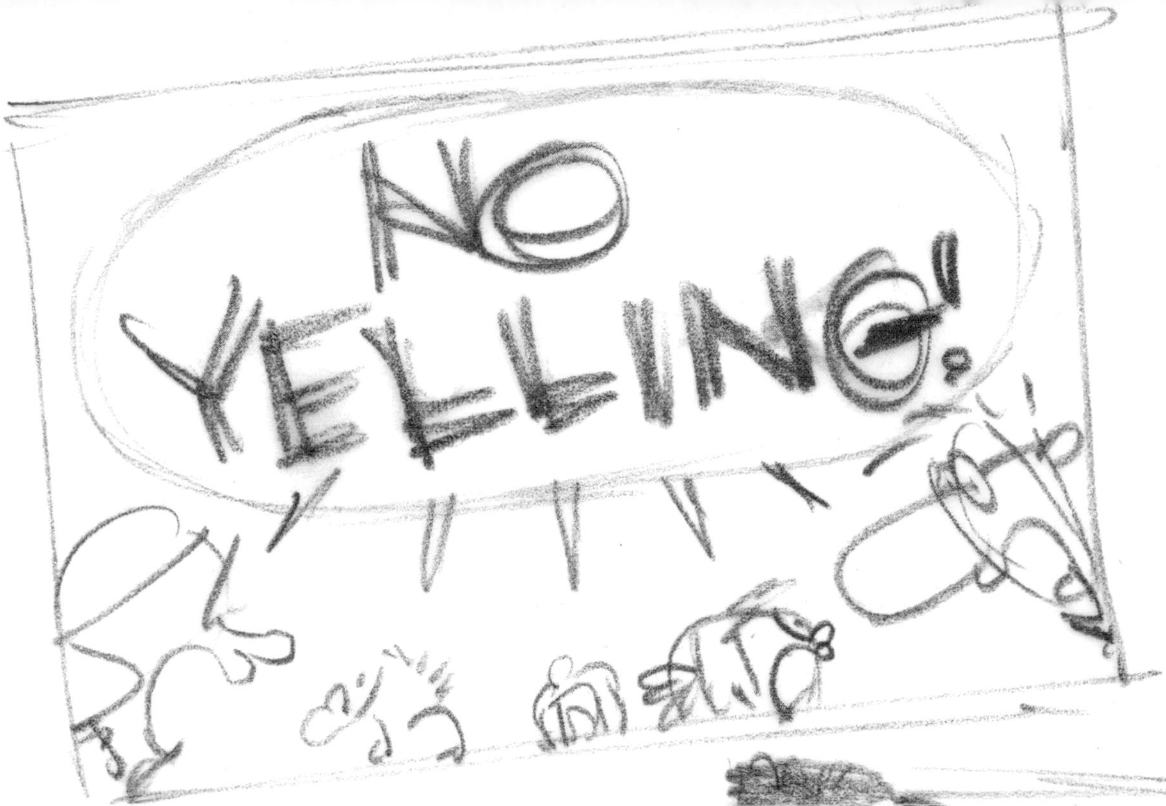
NO YELLING!

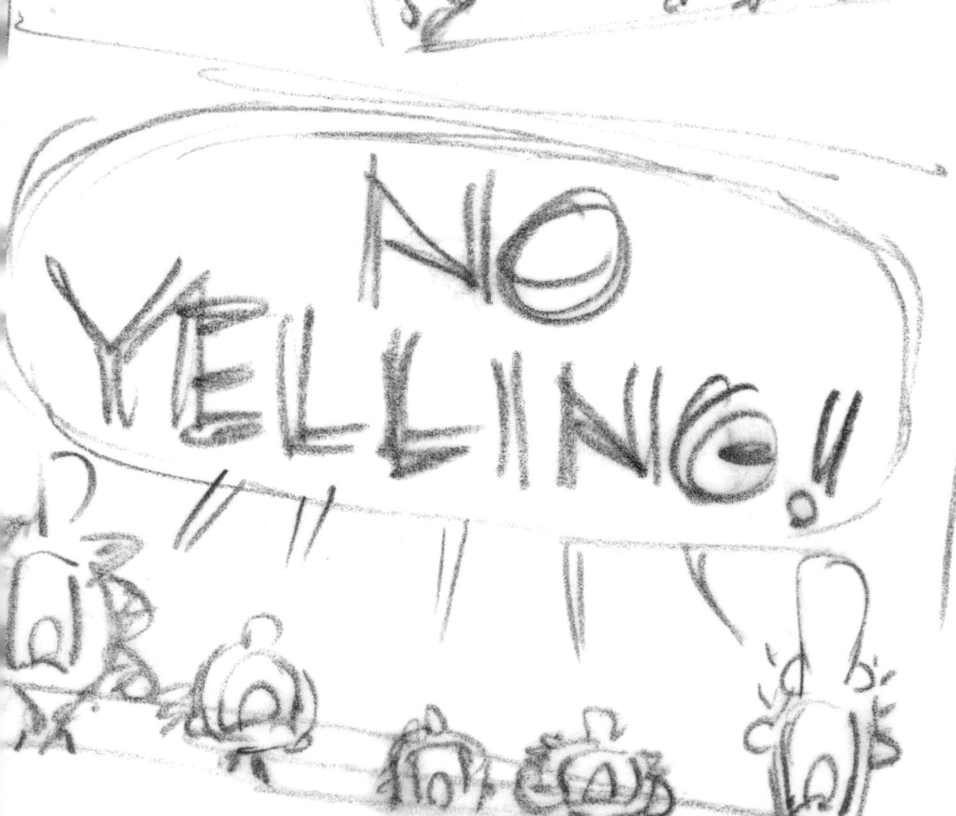
NO YELLING!!

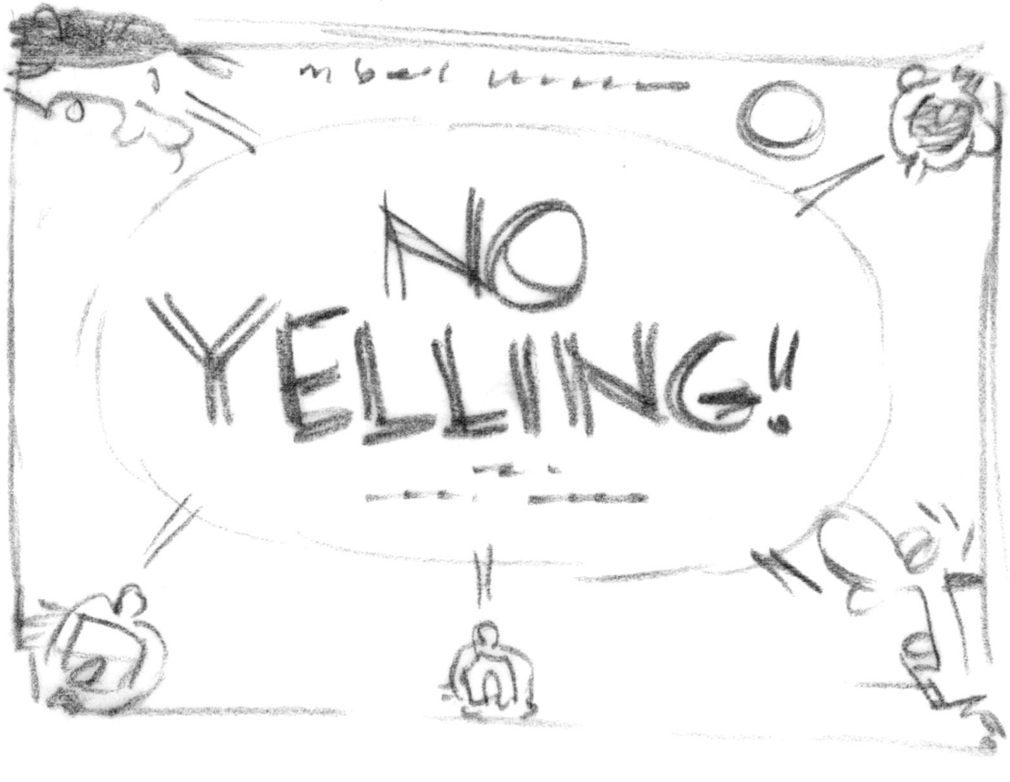
NO YELLING!!

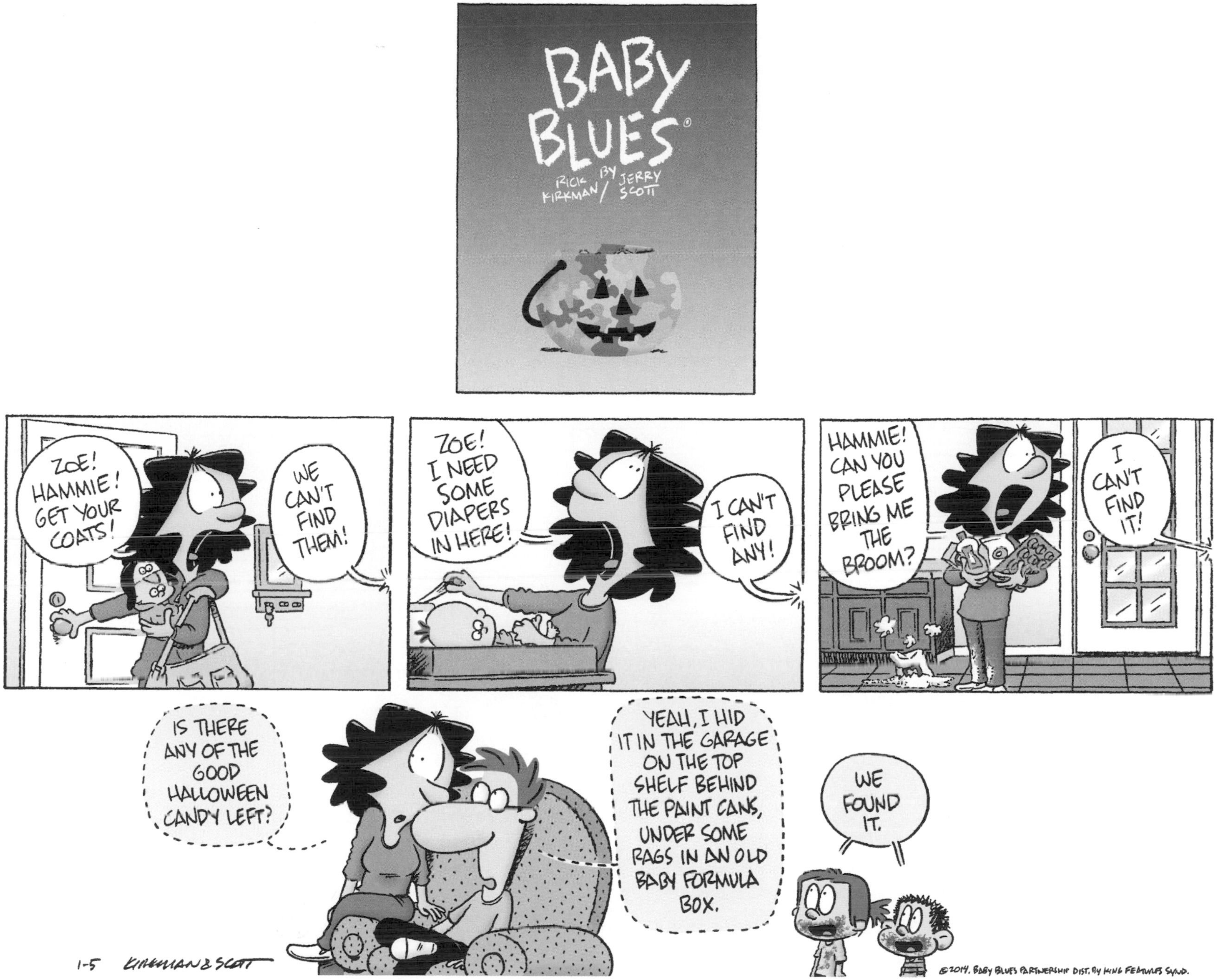
BABY BLUES®
BY RICK KIRKMAN / JERRY SCOTT
ZOE! HAMMIE! GET YOUR COATS!
WE CAN'T FIND THEM!
ZOE! I NEED SOME DIAPERS IN HERE!
I CAN'T FIND ANY!
HAMMIE! CAN YOU PLEASE BRING ME THE BROOM?
I CAN'T FIND IT!
IS THERE ANY OF THE GOOD HALLOWEEN CANDY LEFT?
YEAH, I HID IT IN THE GARAGE ON THE TOP SHELF BEHIND THE PAINT CANS, UNDER SOME RAGS IN AN OLD BABY FORMULA BOX.
WE FOUND IT.
1-5 KIRKMAN & SCOTT
©2014, BABY BLUES PARTNERSHIP DIST. BY KING FEATURES SYND.

Rick: His and Hers Temperature Zones. Please, someone, go out and invent that.

Jerry: I like to talk to people who don't have kids. It's as close as I come to speaking a foreign language.

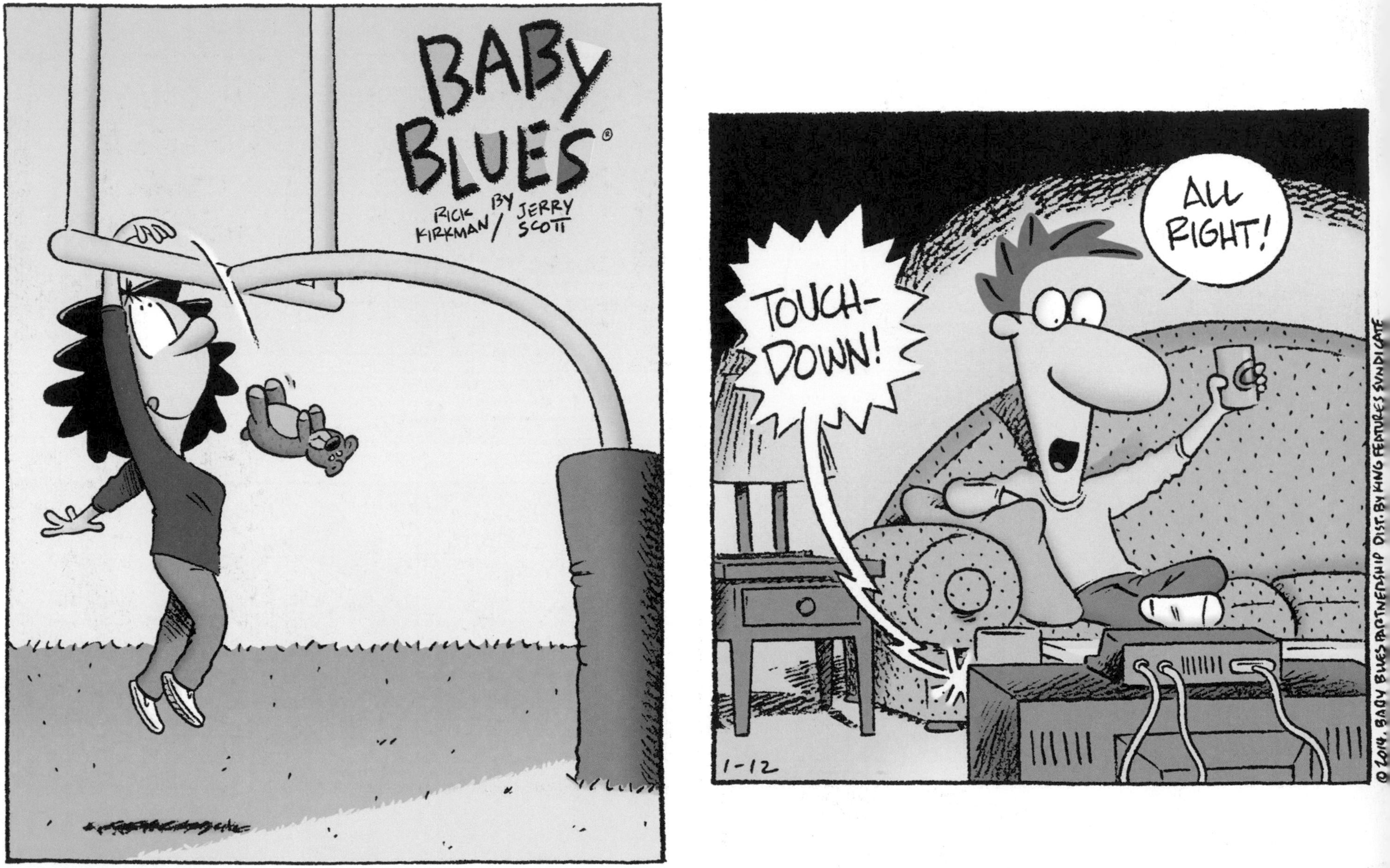
BABY BLUES®
BY RICK KIRKMAN / JERRY SCOTT
TOUCH-DOWN!
ALL RIGHT!
1-12
© 2014, BABY BLUES PARTNERSHIP DIST. BY KING FEATURES SYNDICATE

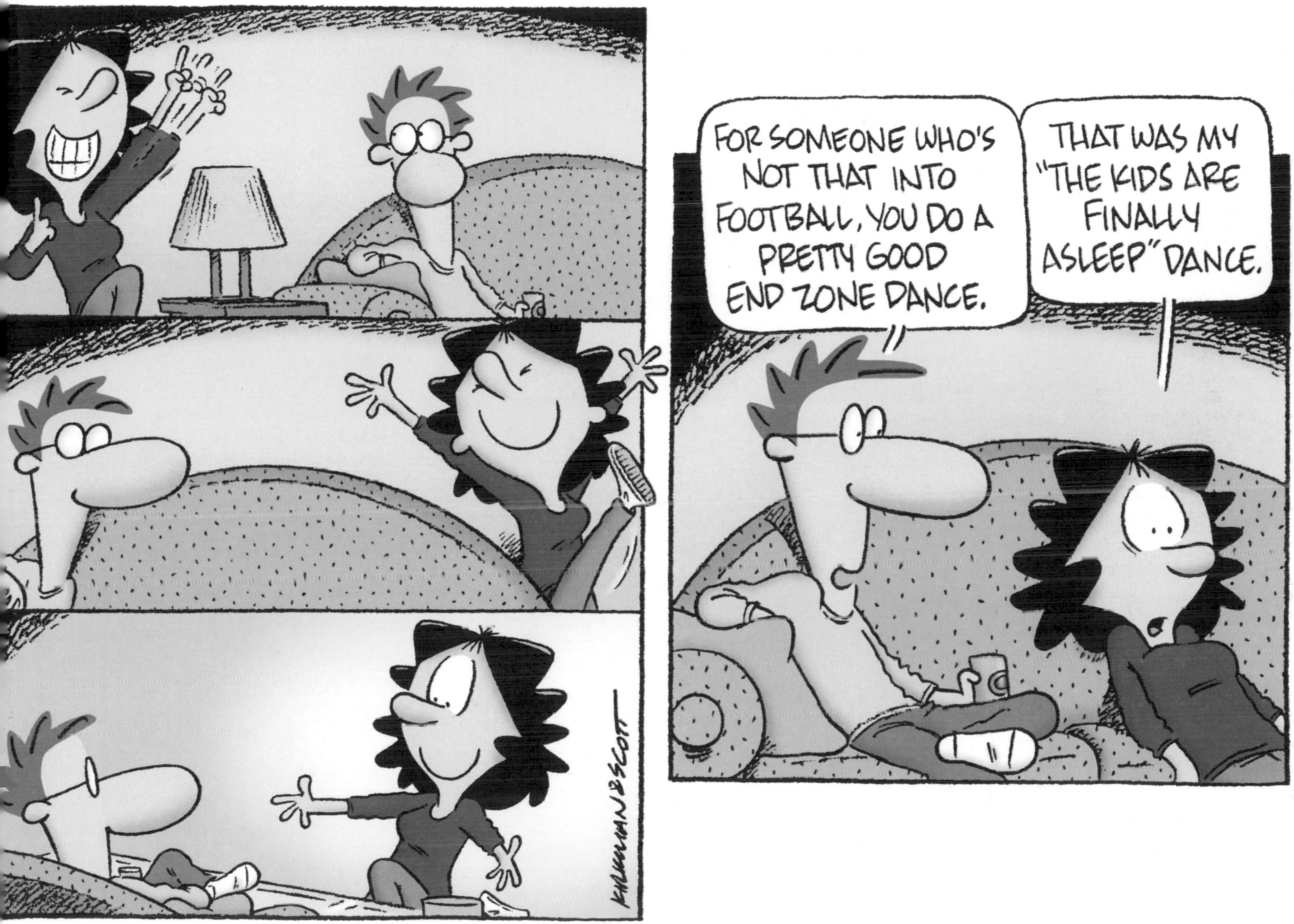
FOR SOMEONE WHO'S NOT THAT INTO FOOTBALL, YOU DO A PRETTY GOOD END ZONE DANCE.
THAT WAS MY "THE KIDS ARE FINALLY ASLEEP" DANCE.
KIRKMAN & SCOTT

Rick: Glory days . . . I never had any, either. I'm still trying to create some, but it's a lost cause.

Rick: Isn't that a parent's job, wringing every cent's worth of value out of everything? I didn't really think of things that way until I had kids.

Jerry: The other day I restricted my kid to using just one iPad at a time. Judging by her reaction, it was a pretty unreasonable punishment.

Jerry: The actual number ended up closer to three and a half zillion.

Rick: That last panel makes me cringe.

Jerry: Little brothers have to use every tool in the annoy-your-sister toolbox.

Rick: A forward-thinking kid can be a wonderful thing, or diabolical.

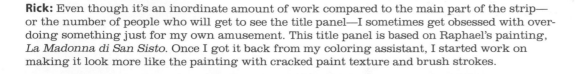

Rick: Even though it's an inordinate amount of work compared to the main part of the strip—or the number of people who will get to see the title panel—I sometimes get obsessed with over-doing something just for my own amusement. This title panel is based on Raphael's painting, *La Madonna di San Sisto*. Once I got it back from my coloring assistant, I started work on making it look more like the painting with cracked paint texture and brush strokes.

Jerry: Newspapers that choose not to run the Sunday title panels are missing out on some great art.

Jerry: If you're gonna ask, ask big.

Rick: Nice thing about having more than one child is the variety. Or extremes.

Jerry: When Rick and I talk to groups, it always surprises me how fast the time goes by. I'm a Zoe.

Rick: Some of my favorite stuff to draw—making faces and sound effects.

Rick: Typical marital nicknames have never been our thing. I just feel silly. The only ones we ever used were creative enough to be used as passwords, though. But then we had to stop using them for each other.

Jerry: Like Darryl and Wanda, my wife and I never got very comfortable with nicknames or endearments. We are on a first-name basis, though.

Rick: Those little routines and rituals really make life complete.

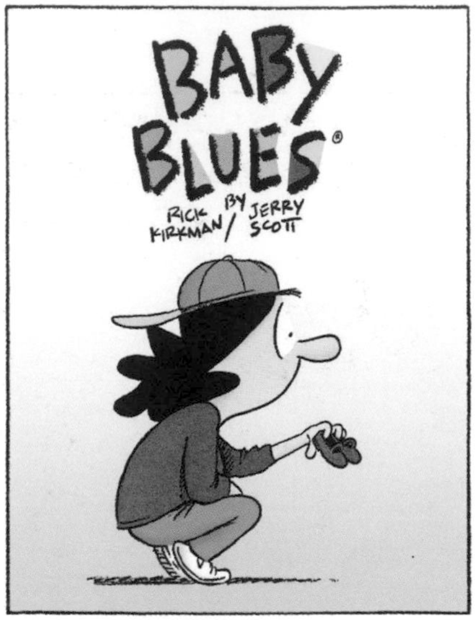
BABY BLUES®
BY RICK KIRKMAN / JERRY SCOTT

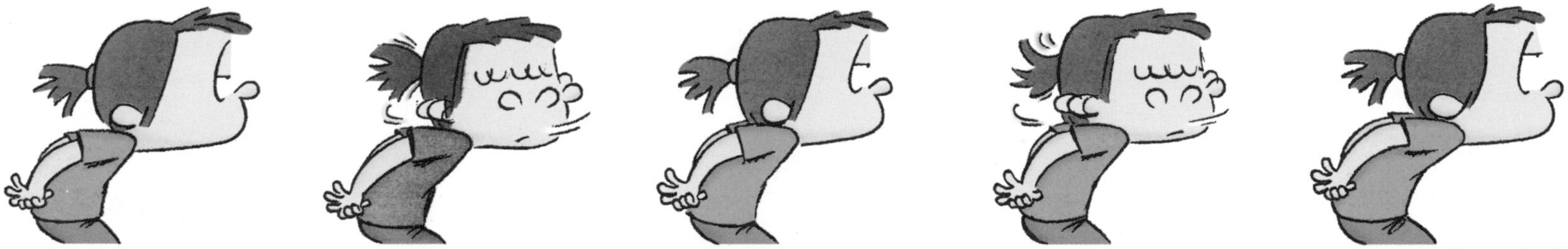

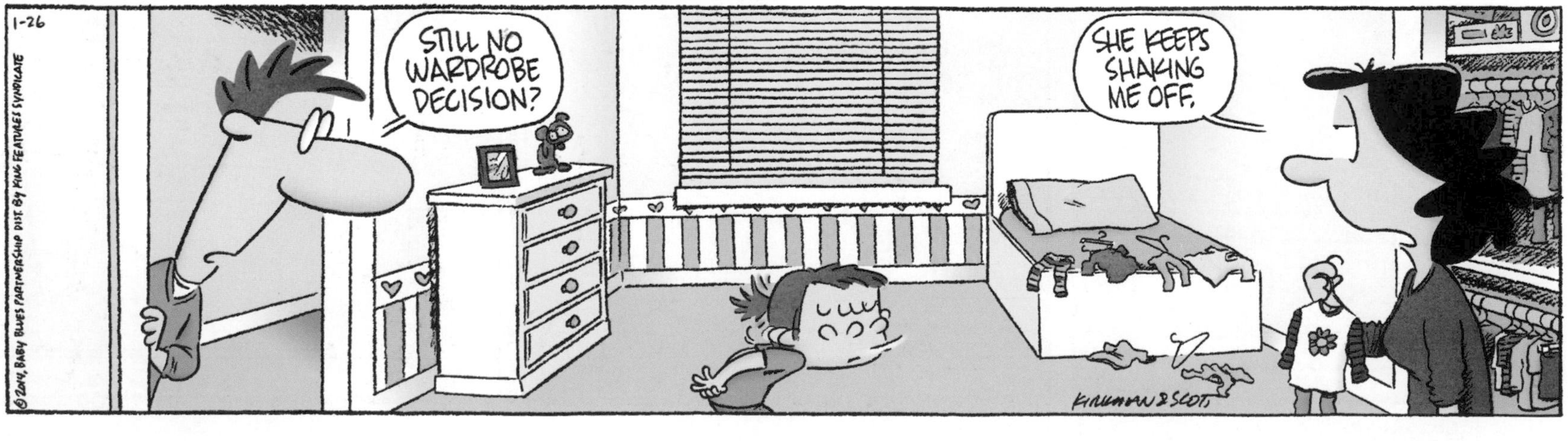
1-26
STILL NO WARDROBE DECISION?
SHE KEEPS SHAKING ME OFF.
© 2014, BABY BLUES PARTNERSHIP DIST. BY KING FEATURES SYNDICATE
KIRKMAN & SCOTT

Rick: Look it up.

Jerry: One of my kids did this once. It got bigger laughs than anything I ever wrote.

Jerry: Kids think they invented everything.

Jerry: We have two cars, and I've never ridden in the backseat of either one for just this reason.

Rick: Only thing worse than the smell of the van of a family with kids would be what's collected in the vacuum from the van of a family with kids.

Jerry: This happened to us once. We had to sell the van quickly and with the windows rolled down.

Jerry: Yeah. There's a lot of that going around.

Rick: Yet another creepy transformation we've put the kids through.

Rick: So the secret to ending selfies is shorter arms? Or will we evolve into having longer arms so we don't need selfie sticks?

Jerry: Teaching the baby to say naughty words is an art form. Just ask my little sister, Soapy-Mouth.

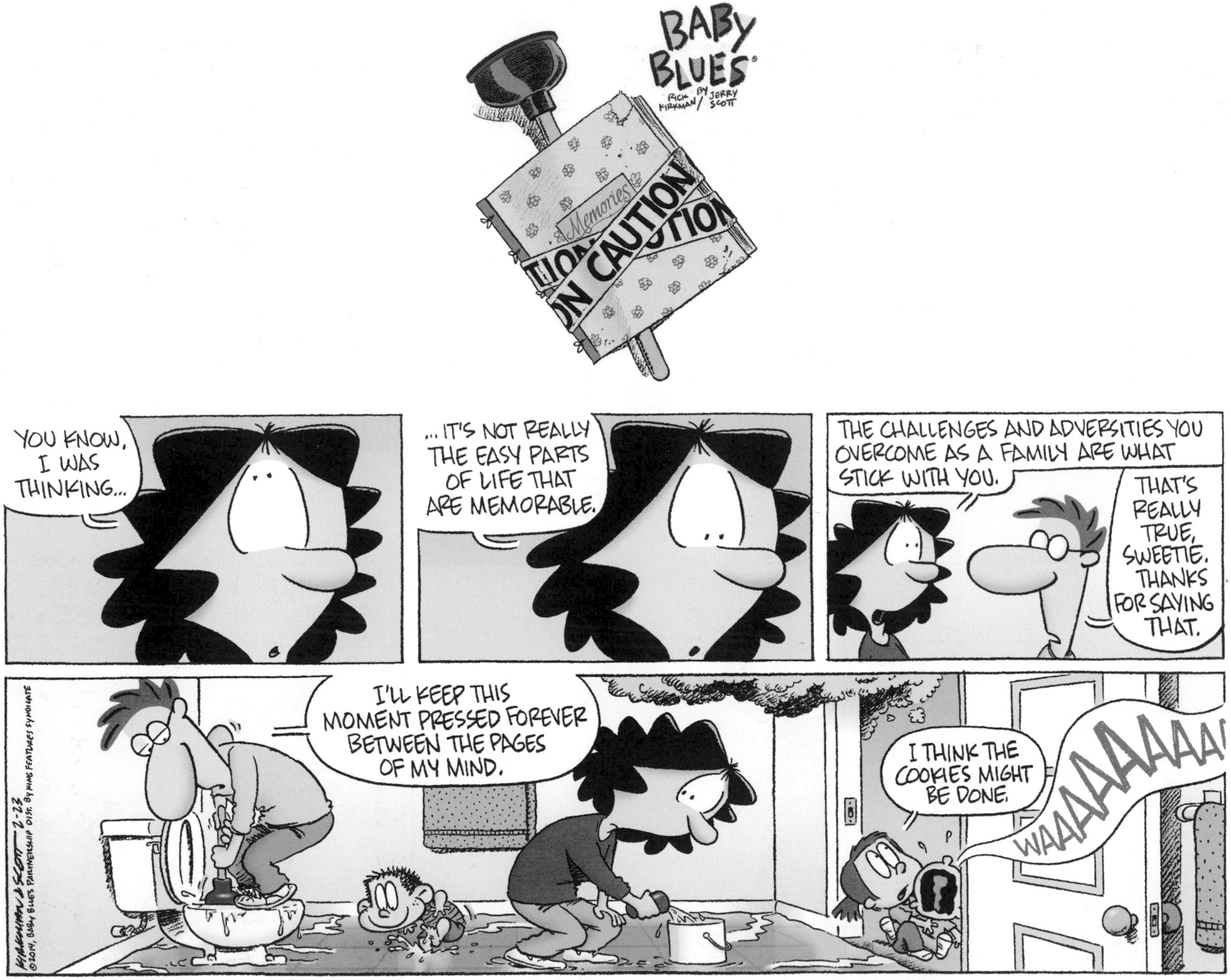
BABY BLUES®
RICK KIRKMAN / BY JERRY SCOTT
Memories
CAUTION
YOU KNOW, I WAS THINKING...
...IT'S NOT REALLY THE EASY PARTS OF LIFE THAT ARE MEMORABLE.
THE CHALLENGES AND ADVERSITIES YOU OVERCOME AS A FAMILY ARE WHAT STICK WITH YOU.
THAT'S REALLY TRUE, SWEETIE. THANKS FOR SAYING THAT.
I'LL KEEP THIS MOMENT PRESSED FOREVER BETWEEN THE PAGES OF MY MIND.
I THINK THE COOKIES MIGHT BE DONE.
WAAAAAAAAA
KIRKMAN & SCOTT 2-23
©2014, BABY BLUES PARTNERSHIP DIST. BY KING FEATURES SYNDICATE

Jerry: I think this is actually kind of true. It's nice when I can share my weirdness with others through the comic strip.

Rick: This one hits a little too close to home for me.

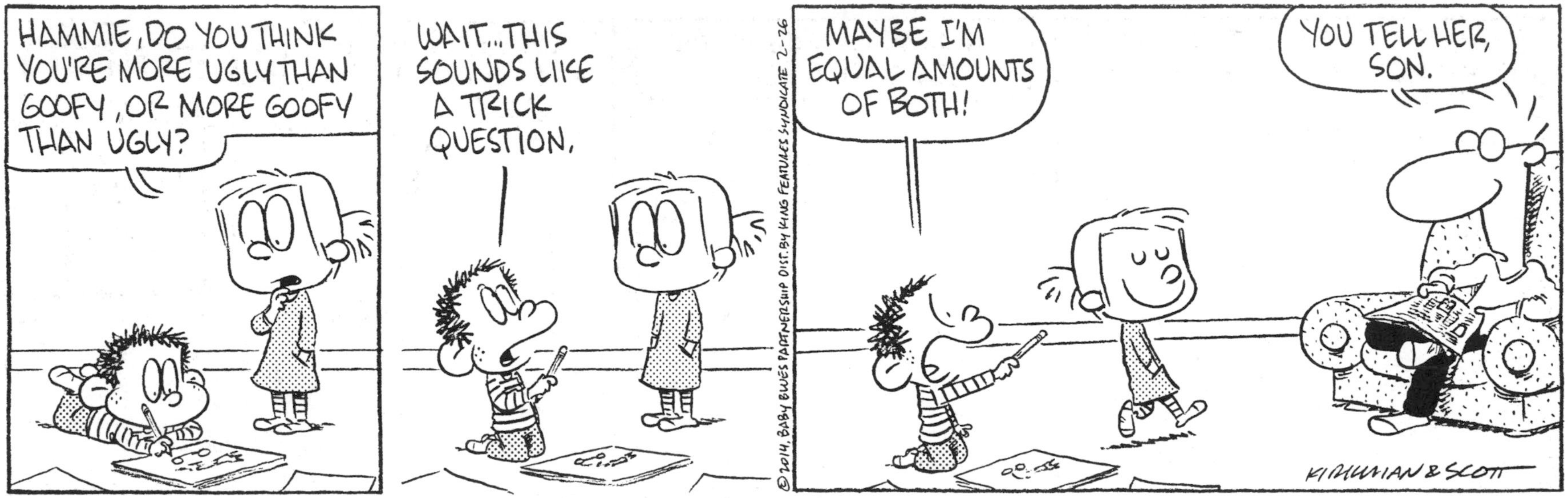
HAMMIE, DO YOU THINK YOU'RE MORE UGLY THAN GOOFY, OR MORE GOOFY THAN UGLY?
WAIT...THIS SOUNDS LIKE A TRICK QUESTION.
© 2014, BABY BLUES PARTNERSHIP DIST. BY KING FEATURES SYNDICATE 2-26
MAYBE I'M EQUAL AMOUNTS OF BOTH!
YOU TELL HER, SON.
KIRKMAN & SCOTT

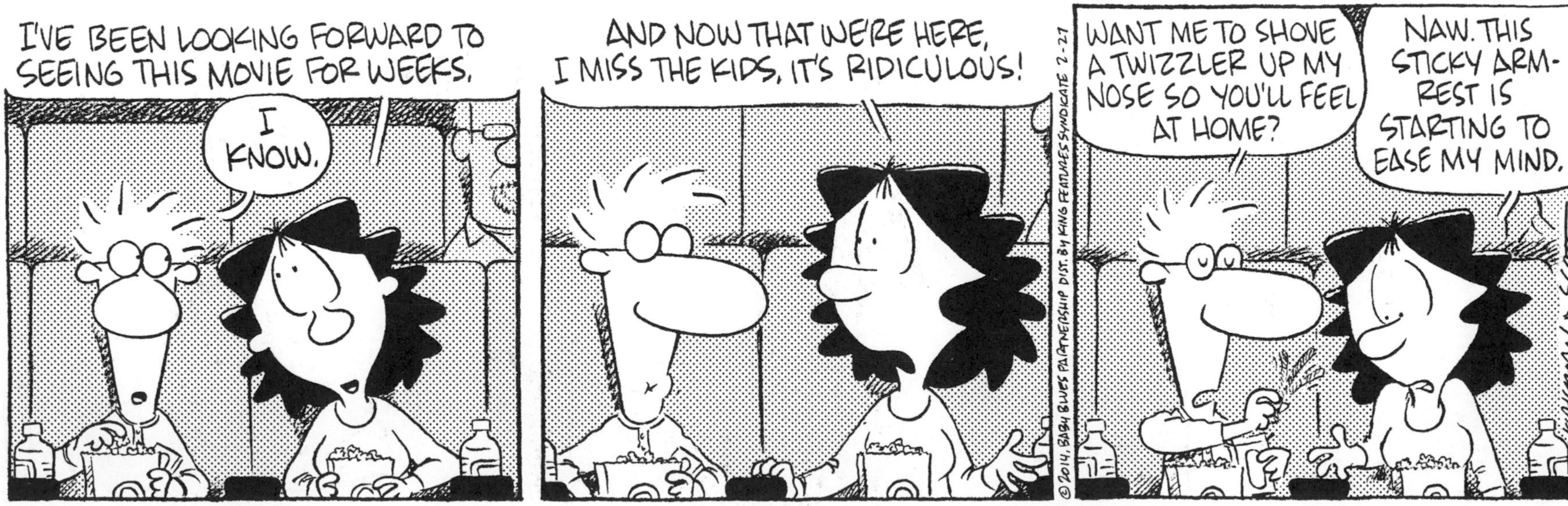
I'VE BEEN LOOKING FORWARD TO SEEING THIS MOVIE FOR WEEKS.
I KNOW.
AND NOW THAT WE'RE HERE, I MISS THE KIDS. IT'S RIDICULOUS!
© 2014, BABY BLUES PARTNERSHIP DIST. BY KING FEATURES SYNDICATE 2-27
WANT ME TO SHOVE A TWIZZLER UP MY NOSE SO YOU'LL FEEL AT HOME?
NAW. THIS STICKY ARM-REST IS STARTING TO EASE MY MIND.
KIRKMAN & SCOTT

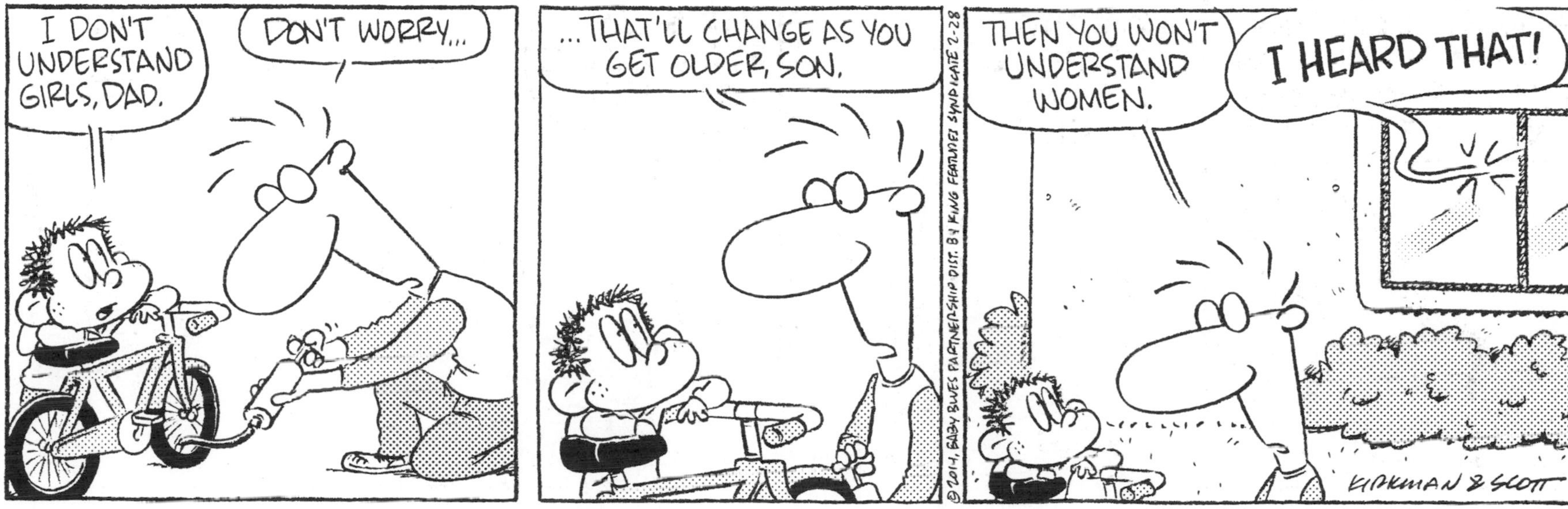
I DON'T UNDERSTAND GIRLS, DAD.
DON'T WORRY...
...THAT'LL CHANGE AS YOU GET OLDER, SON.
© 2014, BABY BLUES PARTNERSHIP DIST. BY KING FEATURES SYNDICATE 2-28
THEN YOU WON'T UNDERSTAND WOMEN.
I HEARD THAT!
KIRKMAN & SCOTT

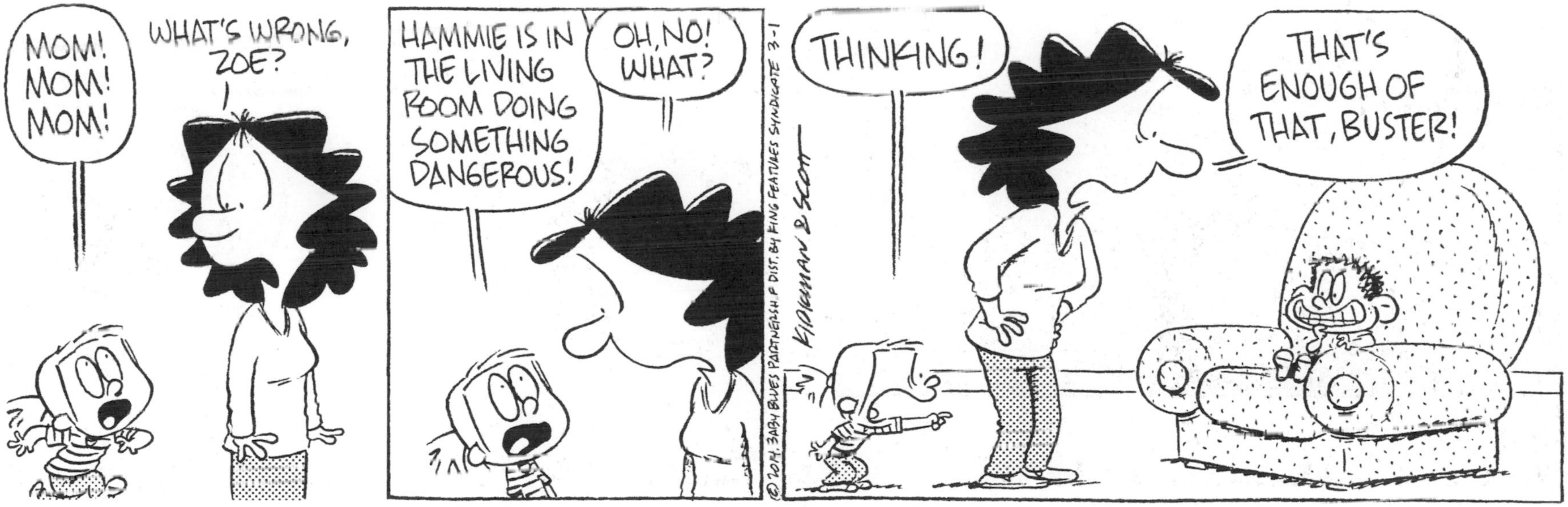
MOM! MOM! MOM!
WHAT'S WRONG, ZOE?
HAMMIE IS IN THE LIVING ROOM DOING SOMETHING DANGEROUS!
OH, NO! WHAT?
© 2014, BABY BLUES PARTNERSHIP DIST. BY KING FEATURES SYNDICATE 3-1
KIRKMAN & SCOTT
THINKING!
THAT'S ENOUGH OF THAT, BUSTER!

Rick: And back to being totally obsessed with a title panel. I was fascinated by how to do her hair to look like the movie poster and re-creating the strip name in the style of *Brave*. Jerry's not kidding about his daughter's hair. It's amazing.

Jerry: Our younger daughter is deeply into Disney princesses. The fact that she has hair like Merida from the movie *Brave* made choosing a Halloween costume really easy that year.

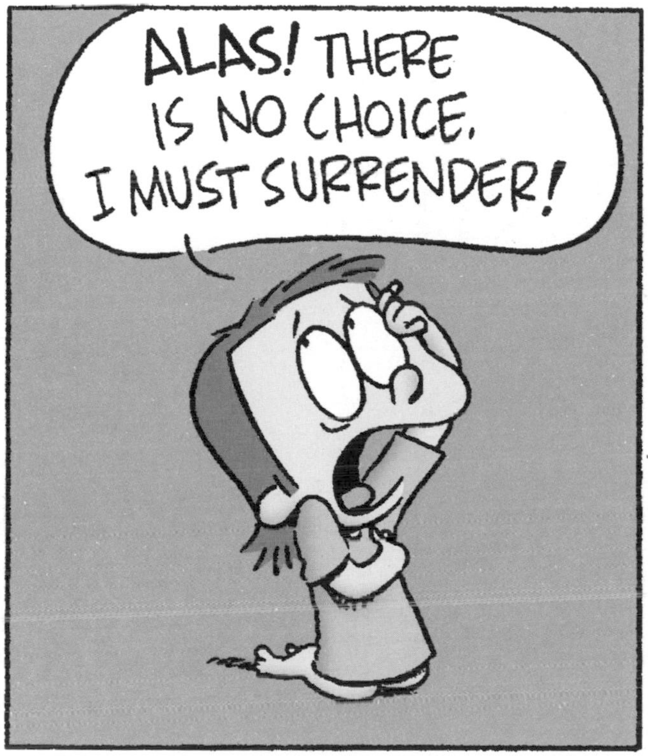
ALAS! THERE IS NO CHOICE. I MUST SURRENDER!

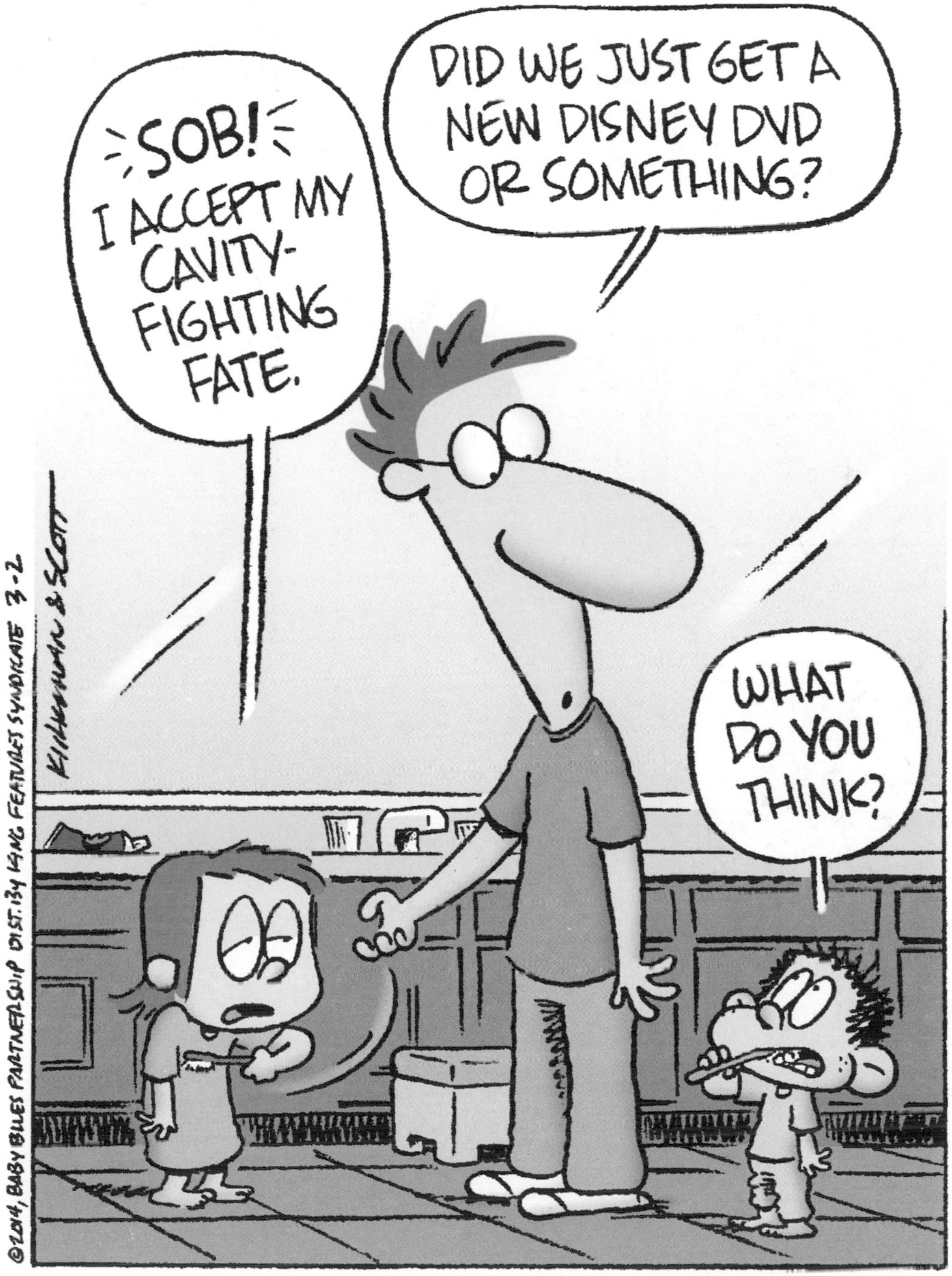
SOB! I ACCEPT MY CAVITY-FIGHTING FATE.
DID WE JUST GET A NEW DISNEY DVD OR SOMETHING?
WHAT DO YOU THINK?
KIRKMAN & SCOTT
©2014, BABY BLUES PARTNERSHIP DIST. BY KING FEATURES SYNDICATE 3-2

Rick: As a freelance illustrator, I used to love to do hand-lettering jobs. This series gave me a chance. I lettered it by hand but wanted to leave it looking a little rough. The "SHAME," if you could see it in its original black version, is hand-lettered, dry-brush style.

Rick: On Darryl's shirt—a tiny nod to the Phoenix Suns, who've made little cameos in the strip over the years.

Rick: That middle panel is just a little bit of heaven for me to do. Love those kinds of drawings.

Jerry: My mom is terrified of snakes. I think that's where Wanda's aversion to them comes from.

Jerry: It's possible that I'm the first person to ever publish the sentence, "My shoes are full of peas!"

Rick: Response time is everything in a situation like that.

Jerry: I visualize the acting when I write these strips, then fuss with the timing of the dialogue. The third panel in this strip made me laugh when I saw it.

Jerry: There's nothing like a habitually naked toddler to keep you on your toes.

Rick: I wanted Wanda's rant to have a continuous feel, but breaking it up into traditional panels didn't lend itself to that. This format allowed both the monologue and the action to flow.

Rick: Ha! Love that answer.

Jerry: Grade school plays are possibly the richest source of kid humor on the planet (especially the really, really bad ones).

Rick: It's such a bonding experience to get Mom involved in your games.

Rick: You can learn just about anything off YouTube, provided you don't get distracted by cat videos, monkey videos, sloth videos, goat videos . . .

Jerry: I have relied on YouTube to learn how to do more things than I care to mention. Or admit to.

Jerry: If you ever want to meet a bunch of hilariously underdressed people, go to a cartoonists convention.

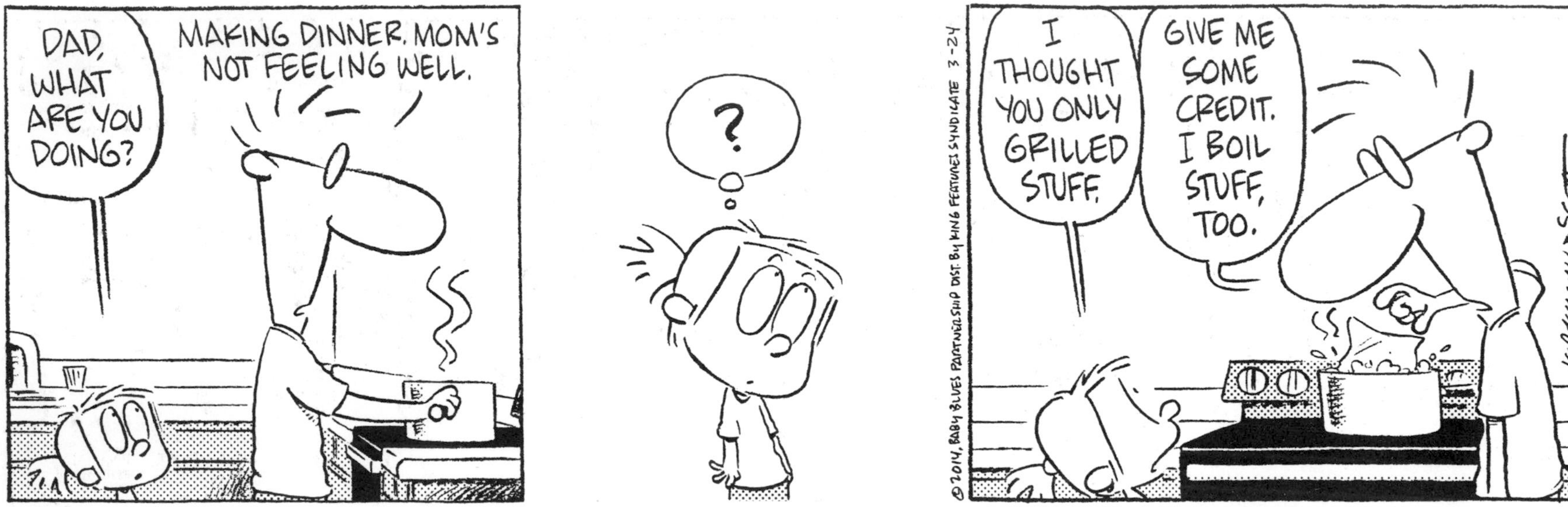
DAD, WHAT ARE YOU DOING?
MAKING DINNER. MOM'S NOT FEELING WELL.
?
I THOUGHT YOU ONLY GRILLED STUFF.
GIVE ME SOME CREDIT. I BOIL STUFF, TOO.
© 2014, BABY BLUES PARTNERSHIP DIST. BY KING FEATURES SYNDICATE 3-24
KIRKMAN & SCOTT

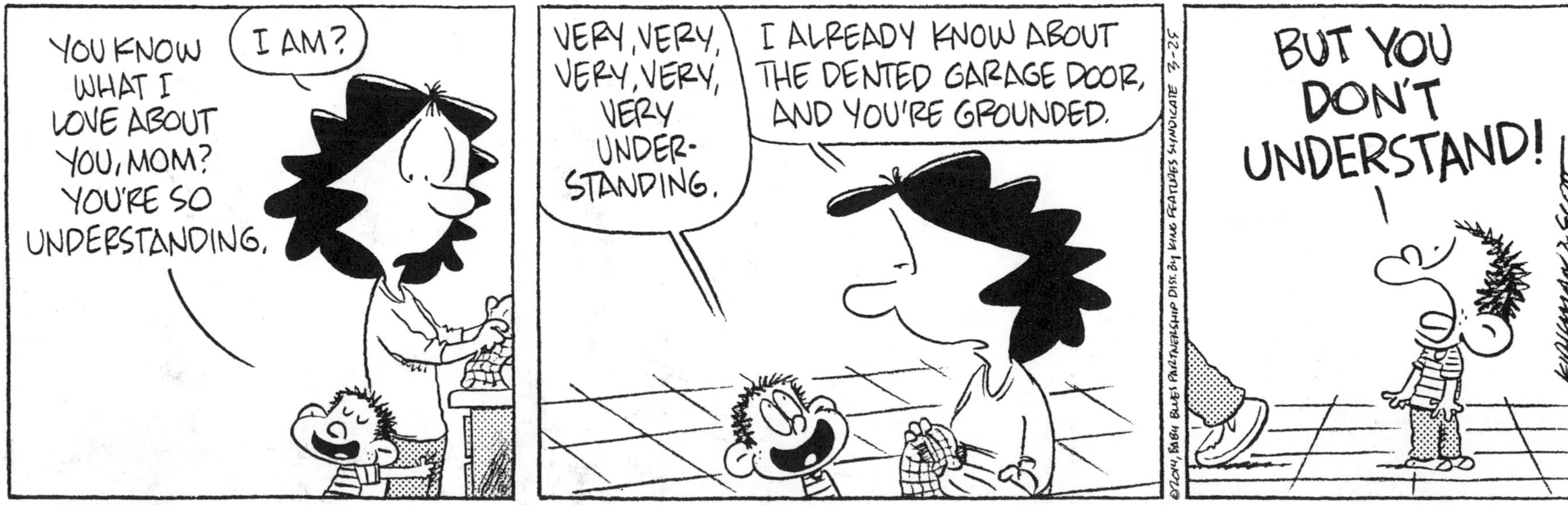
YOU KNOW WHAT I LOVE ABOUT YOU, MOM? YOU'RE SO UNDERSTANDING.
I AM?
VERY, VERY, VERY, VERY, VERY UNDER-STANDING.
I ALREADY KNOW ABOUT THE DENTED GARAGE DOOR, AND YOU'RE GROUNDED.
©2014, BABY BLUES PARTNERSHIP DIST. BY KING FEATURES SYNDICATE 3-25
BUT YOU DON'T UNDERSTAND!
KIRKMAN & SCOTT

Jerry: Understandable.

Jerry: "Mom" is still my mom's name. At least nobody told me if she changed it back to Peggy.

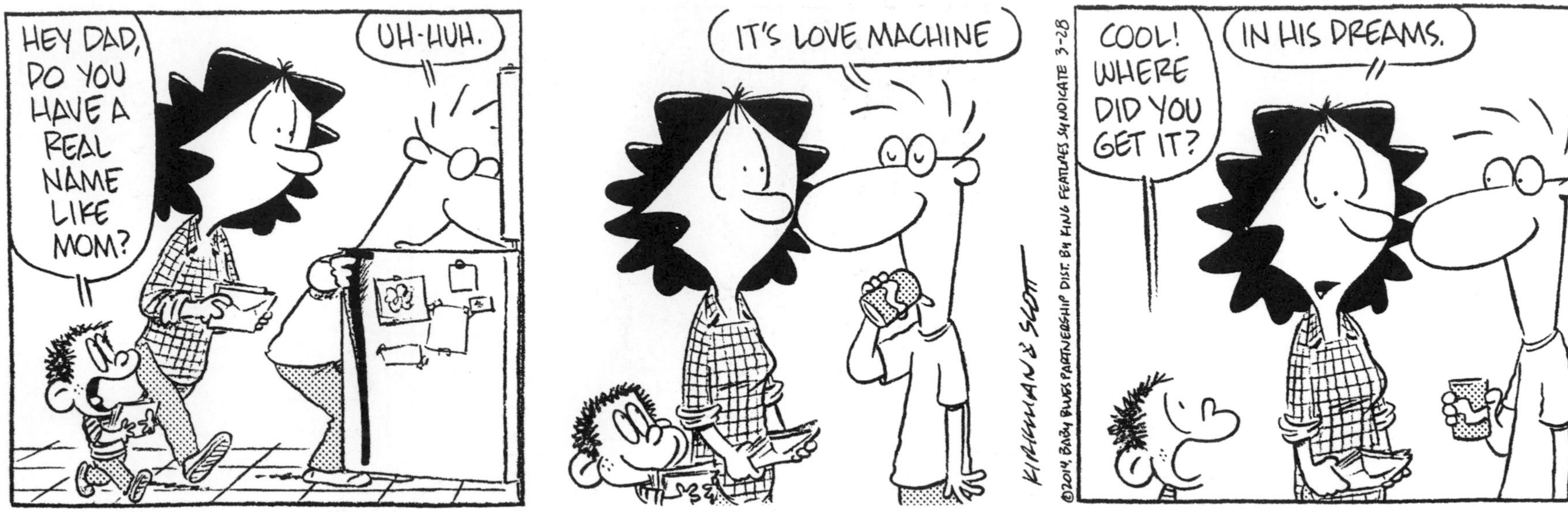
HEY DAD, DO YOU HAVE A REAL NAME LIKE MOM?
UH-HUH.
IT'S LOVE MACHINE
COOL! WHERE DID YOU GET IT?
IN HIS DREAMS.
KIRKMAN & SCOTT
©2014, BABY BLUES PARTNERSHIP DIST. BY KING FEATURES SYNDICATE 3-28

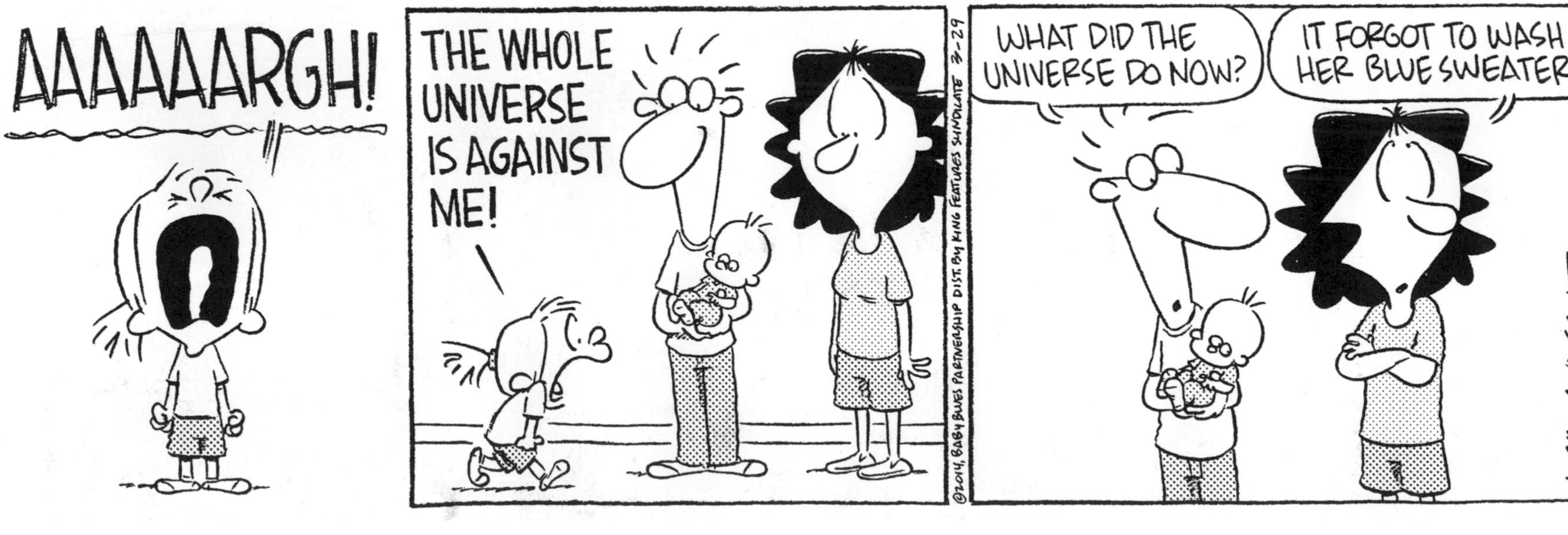
AAAAAARGH!
THE WHOLE UNIVERSE IS AGAINST ME!
©2014, BABY BLUES PARTNERSHIP DIST. BY KING FEATURES SYNDICATE 3-29
WHAT DID THE UNIVERSE DO NOW?
IT FORGOT TO WASH HER BLUE SWEATER.
KIRKMAN & SCOTT

Rick: I will look back on 2014 as "The Year of Title Panel Obsession." This time: Super Mario Bros.

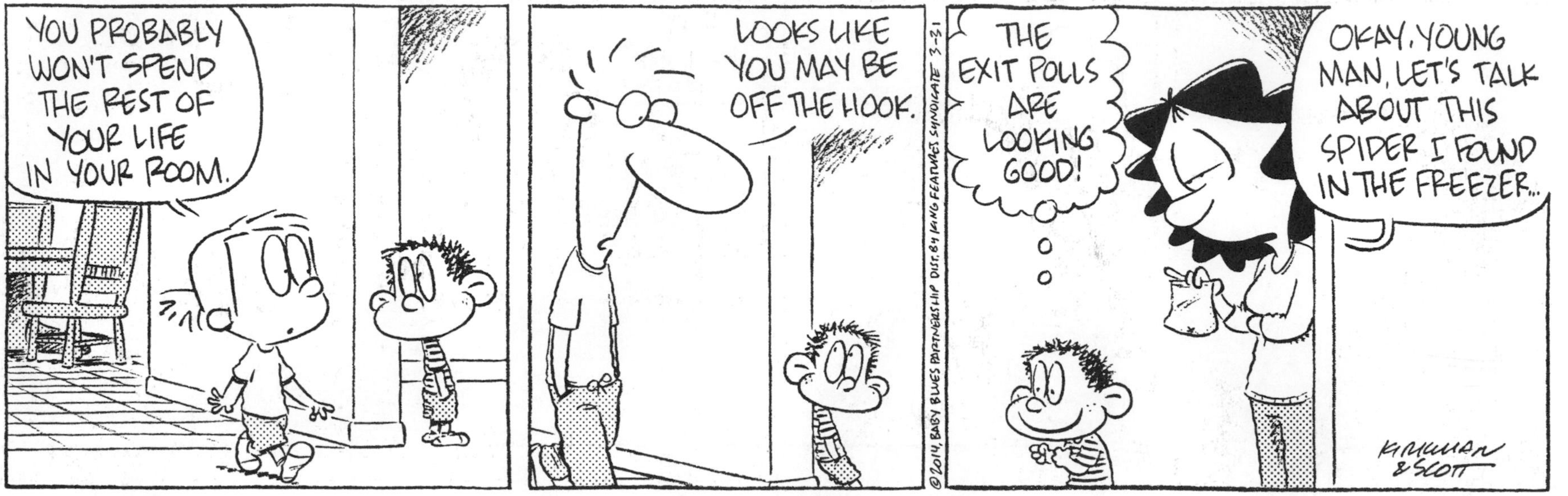
YOU PROBABLY WON'T SPEND THE REST OF YOUR LIFE IN YOUR ROOM.
LOOKS LIKE YOU MAY BE OFF THE HOOK.
© 2014, BABY BLUES PARTNERSHIP DIST. BY KING FEATURES SYNDICATE 3-31
THE EXIT POLLS ARE LOOKING GOOD!
OKAY, YOUNG MAN, LET'S TALK ABOUT THIS SPIDER I FOUND IN THE FREEZER...
KIRKMAN & SCOTT

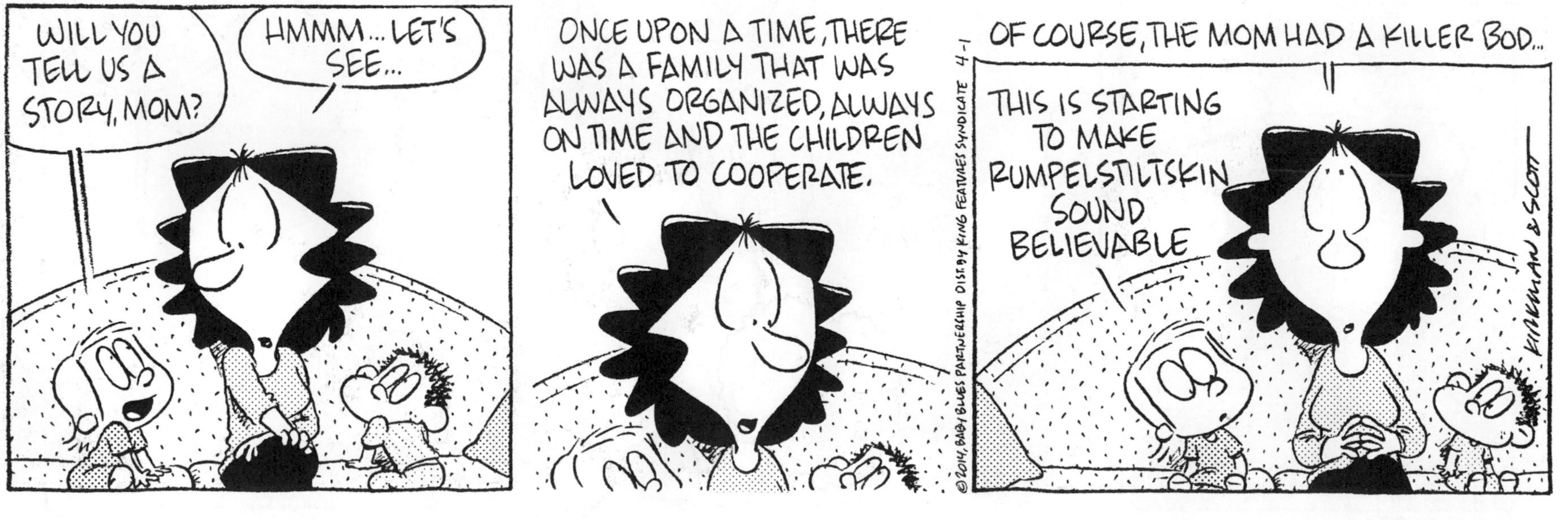
WILL YOU TELL US A STORY, MOM?
HMMM... LET'S SEE...
ONCE UPON A TIME, THERE WAS A FAMILY THAT WAS ALWAYS ORGANIZED, ALWAYS ON TIME AND THE CHILDREN LOVED TO COOPERATE.
© 2014, BABY BLUES PARTNERSHIP DIST. BY KING FEATURES SYNDICATE 4-1
OF COURSE, THE MOM HAD A KILLER BOD...
THIS IS STARTING TO MAKE RUMPELSTILTSKIN SOUND BELIEVABLE
KIRKMAN & SCOTT

Jerry: Our younger daughter holds the record for Slowest Game Ever at Pismo Bowl. And it was only three frames.

Rick: Side note: You'd think after three kids, Wanda would know better than to do that with Wren.

Jerry: One of life's great pleasures is getting away with something by following instructions to the letter.

Rick: If you can't beat 'em, trick 'em.

Rick: Here was an opportunity to play with the layout. The last panel needed a lot of horizontal space. Luckily, the panel ahead of it also lent itself to being horizontal. Love the word "SPANG!" too.

Rick: Is that a misspelling? Shouldn't it be "tattletale"? Looks like we all dropped the ball on that one.

Jerry: When Hammie is annoying his sisters, you can be pretty sure that I've been thinking about my childhood.

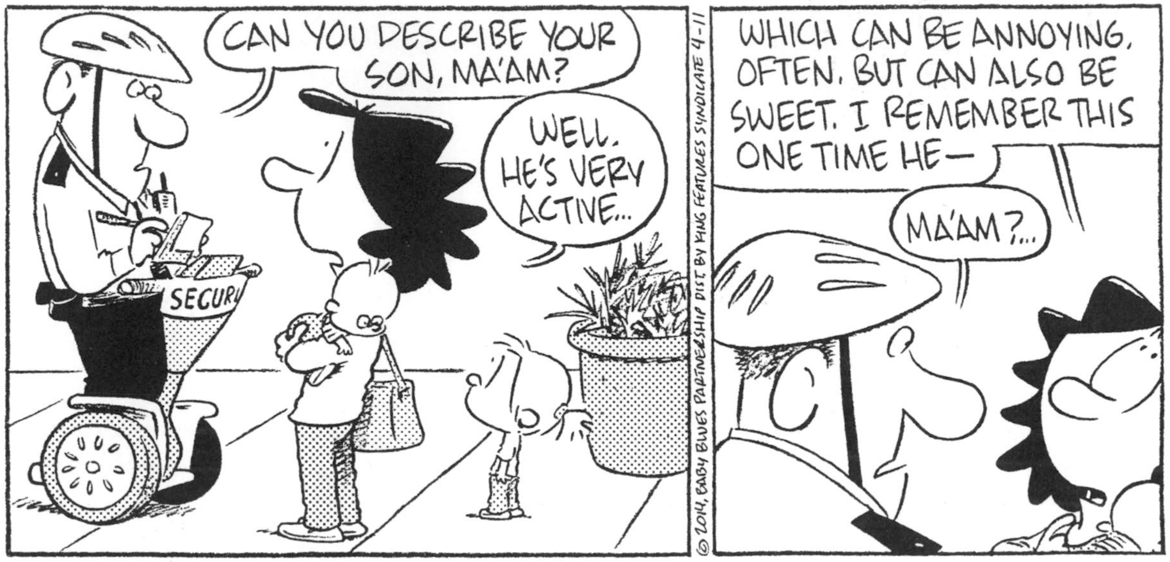
CAN YOU DESCRIBE YOUR SON, MA'AM?
WELL. HE'S VERY ACTIVE...
© 2014, BABY BLUES PARTNERSHIP DIST. BY KING FEATURES SYNDICATE 4-11
WHICH CAN BE ANNOYING, OFTEN. BUT CAN ALSO BE SWEET. I REMEMBER THIS ONE TIME HE—
MA'AM?...
MAYBE YOU COULD JUST TELL ME WHAT HE WAS WEARING.
OH. PROBABLY SOMETHING DIRT-COLORED AND STICKY.
KIRKMAN & SCOTT

Rick: Sorry, but Segways are funny.

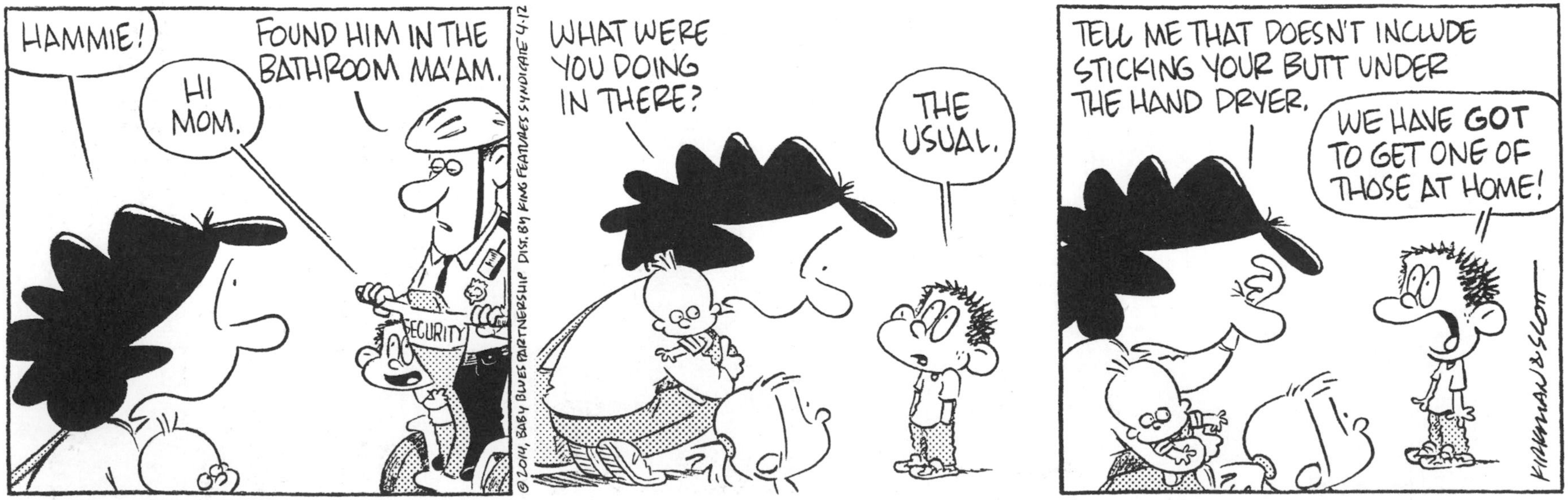
HAMMIE!
HI MOM.
FOUND HIM IN THE BATHROOM MA'AM.
SECURITY
© 2014, BABY BLUES PARTNERSHIP DIST. BY KING FEATURES SYNDICATE 4-12
WHAT WERE YOU DOING IN THERE?
THE USUAL.
TELL ME THAT DOESN'T INCLUDE STICKING YOUR BUTT UNDER THE HAND DRYER.
WE HAVE **GOT** TO GET ONE OF THOSE AT HOME!
KIRKMAN & SCOTT

Rick: True story. Not exactly *House Beautiful* material.

Rick: A nurse midwife wrote to tell us that this strip was being displayed at their clinic on their lactation board.

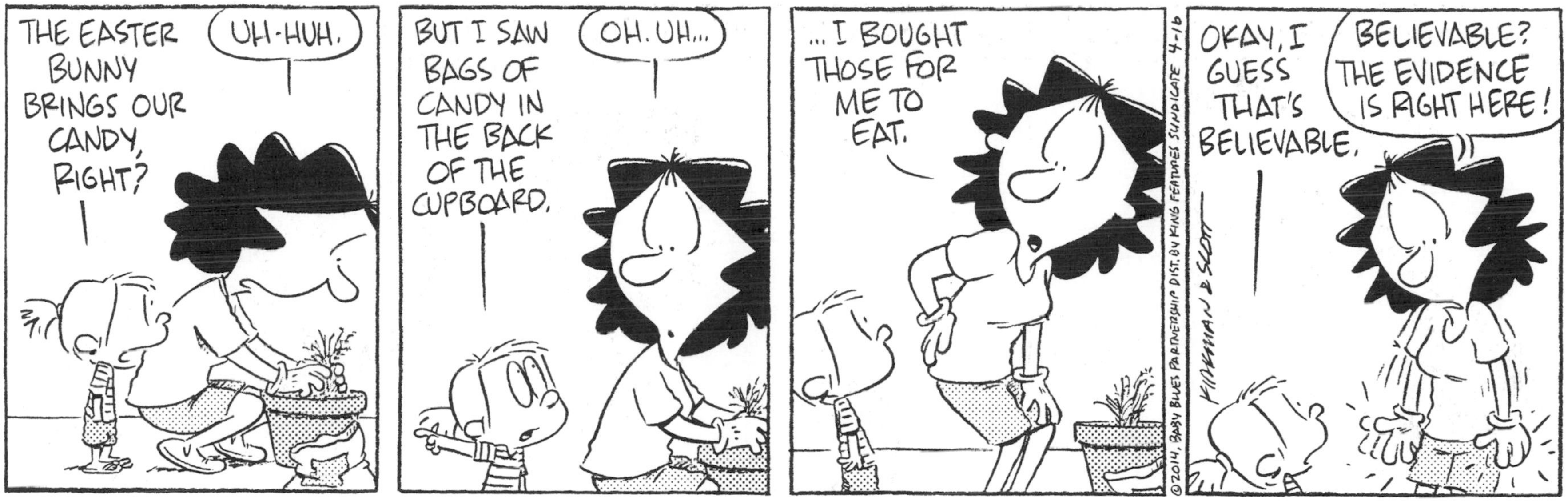
THE EASTER BUNNY BRINGS OUR CANDY, RIGHT?
UH-HUH.
BUT I SAW BAGS OF CANDY IN THE BACK OF THE CUPBOARD.
OH. UH...
...I BOUGHT THOSE FOR ME TO EAT.
OKAY, I GUESS THAT'S BELIEVABLE.
BELIEVABLE? THE EVIDENCE IS RIGHT HERE!

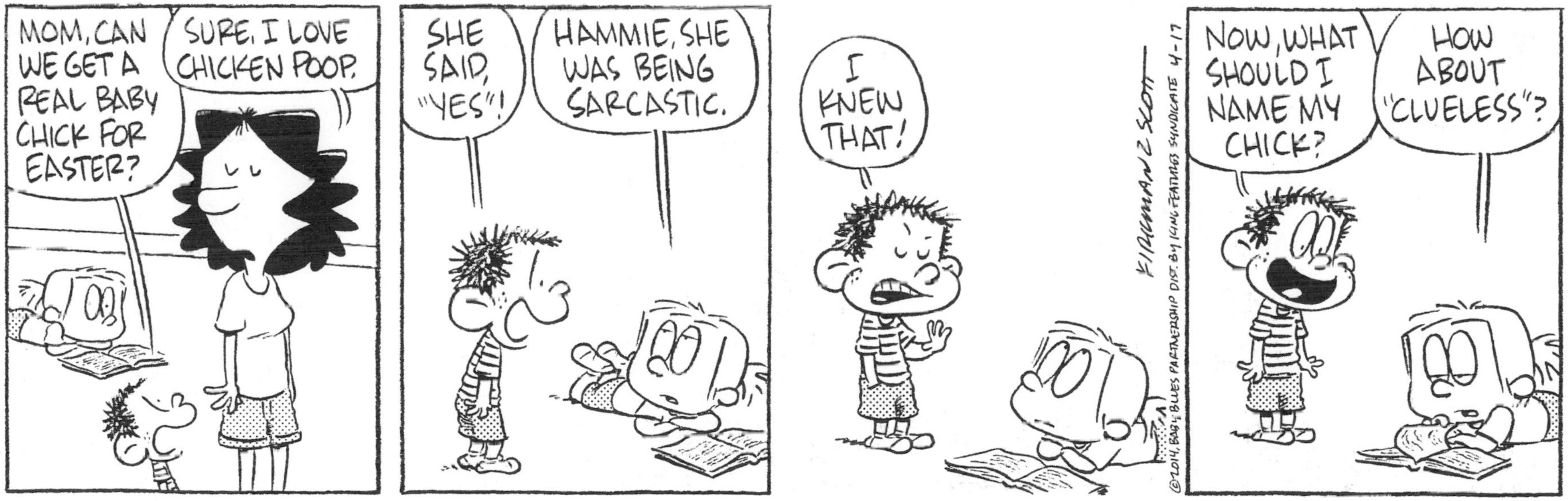
MOM, CAN WE GET A REAL BABY CHICK FOR EASTER?
SURE. I LOVE CHICKEN POOP.
SHE SAID, "YES"!
HAMMIE, SHE WAS BEING SARCASTIC.
I KNEW THAT!
NOW, WHAT SHOULD I NAME MY CHICK?
HOW ABOUT "CLUELESS"?

Rick: I love this one.

Rick: Hmm . . . how to draw the interior of a home-improvement warehouse store, and still be able to read the dialogue and see the characters in a panel the size of a candy bar? Leave out just about everything, and keep a few things as shorthand: A/C unit on a pallet, Rhino Rack shelving, some power and hand tools. Still, the trap box is a little too small. *sigh*

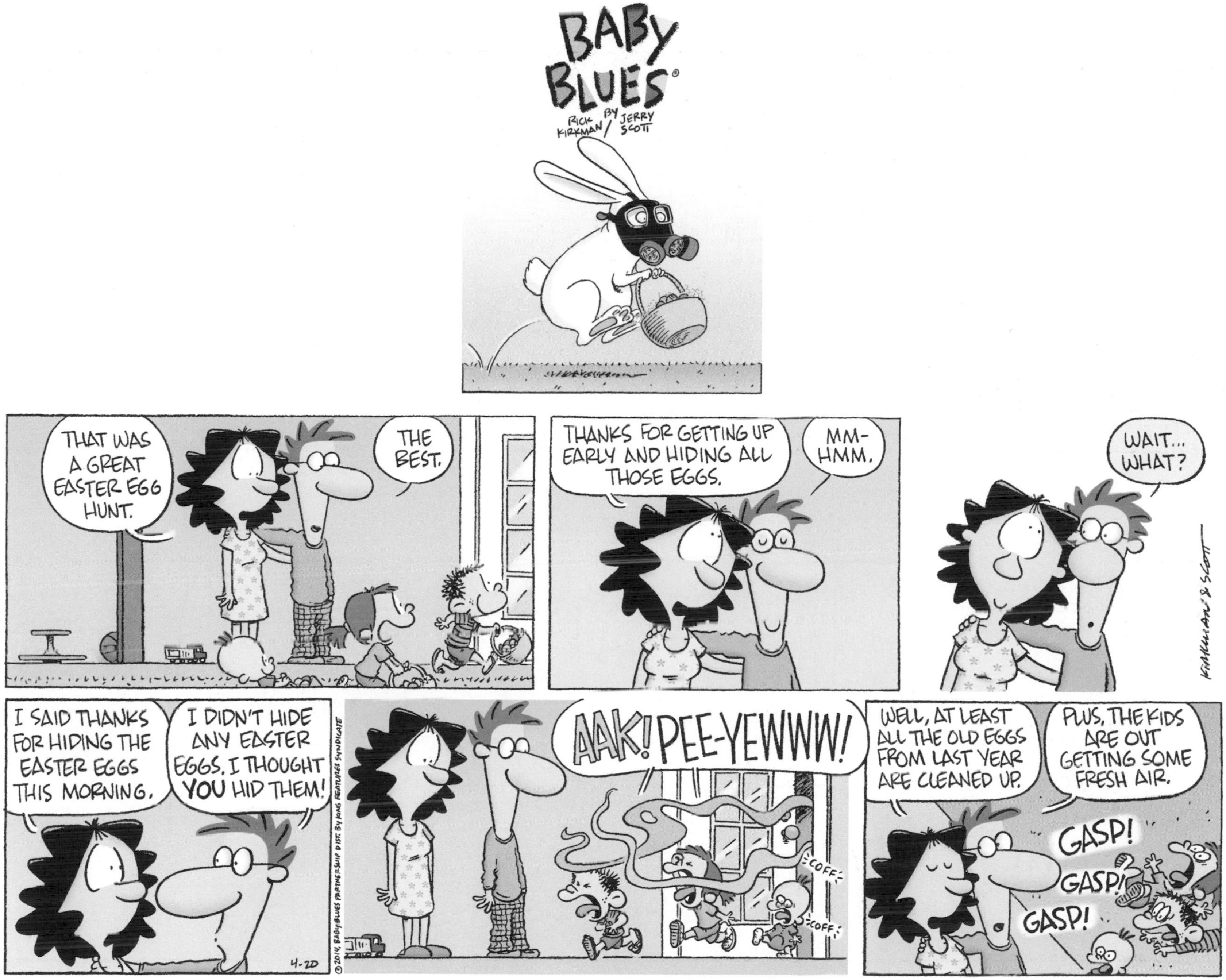
BABY BLUES®
BY RICK KIRKMAN / JERRY SCOTT
THAT WAS A GREAT EASTER EGG HUNT.
THE BEST.
THANKS FOR GETTING UP EARLY AND HIDING ALL THOSE EGGS.
MM-HMM.
WAIT... WHAT?
KIRKMAN & SCOTT
I SAID THANKS FOR HIDING THE EASTER EGGS THIS MORNING.
I DIDN'T HIDE ANY EASTER EGGS. I THOUGHT YOU HID THEM!
4-20
© 2014, BABY BLUES PARTNERSHIP DIST. BY KING FEATURES SYNDICATE
AAK! PEE-YEWWW!
COFF
COFF
WELL, AT LEAST ALL THE OLD EGGS FROM LAST YEAR ARE CLEANED UP.
PLUS, THE KIDS ARE OUT GETTING SOME FRESH AIR.
GASP!
GASP!
GASP!

Jerry: Never lend your good tools to your kids for craft projects. For a while I had a hammer that looked like something you'd find on Elton John's workbench.

Rick: My kids may not have actually said that, but I've seen it in their eyes.

Rick: Now that's a Universal Truth.

Rick: Universal Truth Number 2.

Jerry: Zoe's optimism about getting a pony is kind of inspiring. You gotta' believe.

Jerry: Wrangling kids and running errands can put some CrossFit workouts to shame.

Rick: Oh, if only that could be patented.

Jerry: Sometimes not showing what's going on is funnier than showing it.

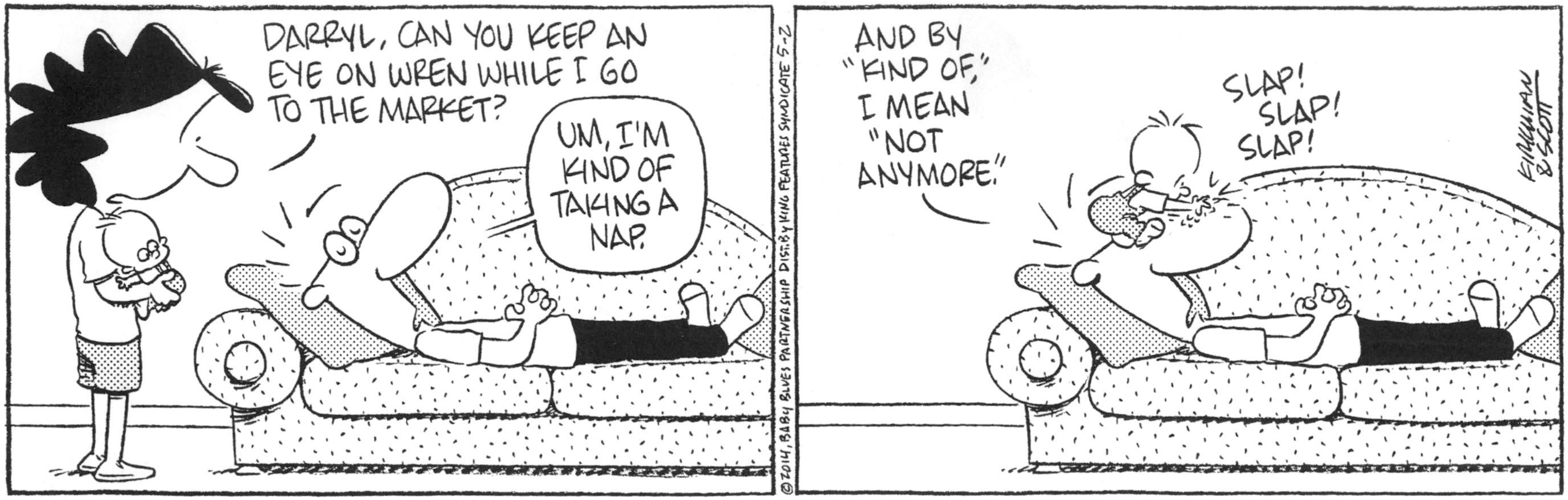
DARRYL, CAN YOU KEEP AN EYE ON WREN WHILE I GO TO THE MARKET?
UM, I'M KIND OF TAKING A NAP.
©2014, BABY BLUES PARTNERSHIP DIST. BY KING FEATURES SYNDICATE 5-2
AND BY "KIND OF," I MEAN "NOT ANYMORE."
SLAP! SLAP! SLAP!
KIRKMAN & SCOTT

Jerry: Flexibility is the key to a good marriage like Darryl's and Wanda's.

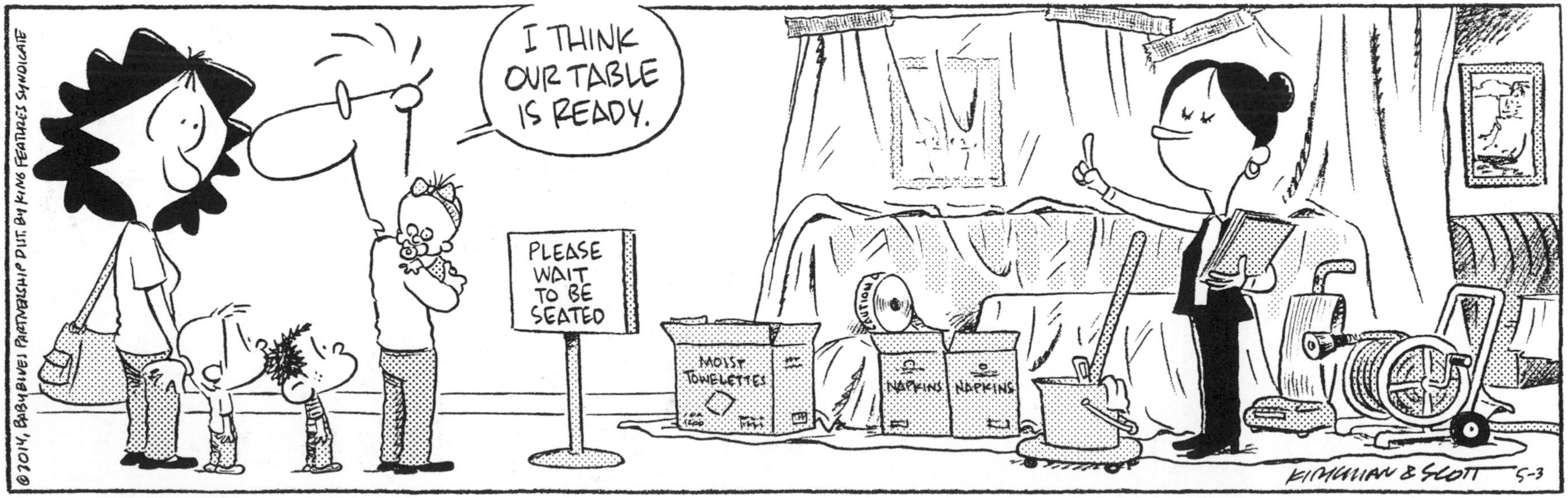
©2014, BABY BLUES PARTNERSHIP DIST. BY KING FEATURES SYNDICATE
I THINK OUR TABLE IS READY.
PLEASE WAIT TO BE SEATED
CAUTION
MOIST TOWELETTES
NAPKINS
NAPKINS
KIRKMAN & SCOTT 5-3

Rick: If this were a crime movie, and the characters walked into a room covered in plastic sheeting, that would be foreshadowing. In the MacPhersons' case it's S.O.P.

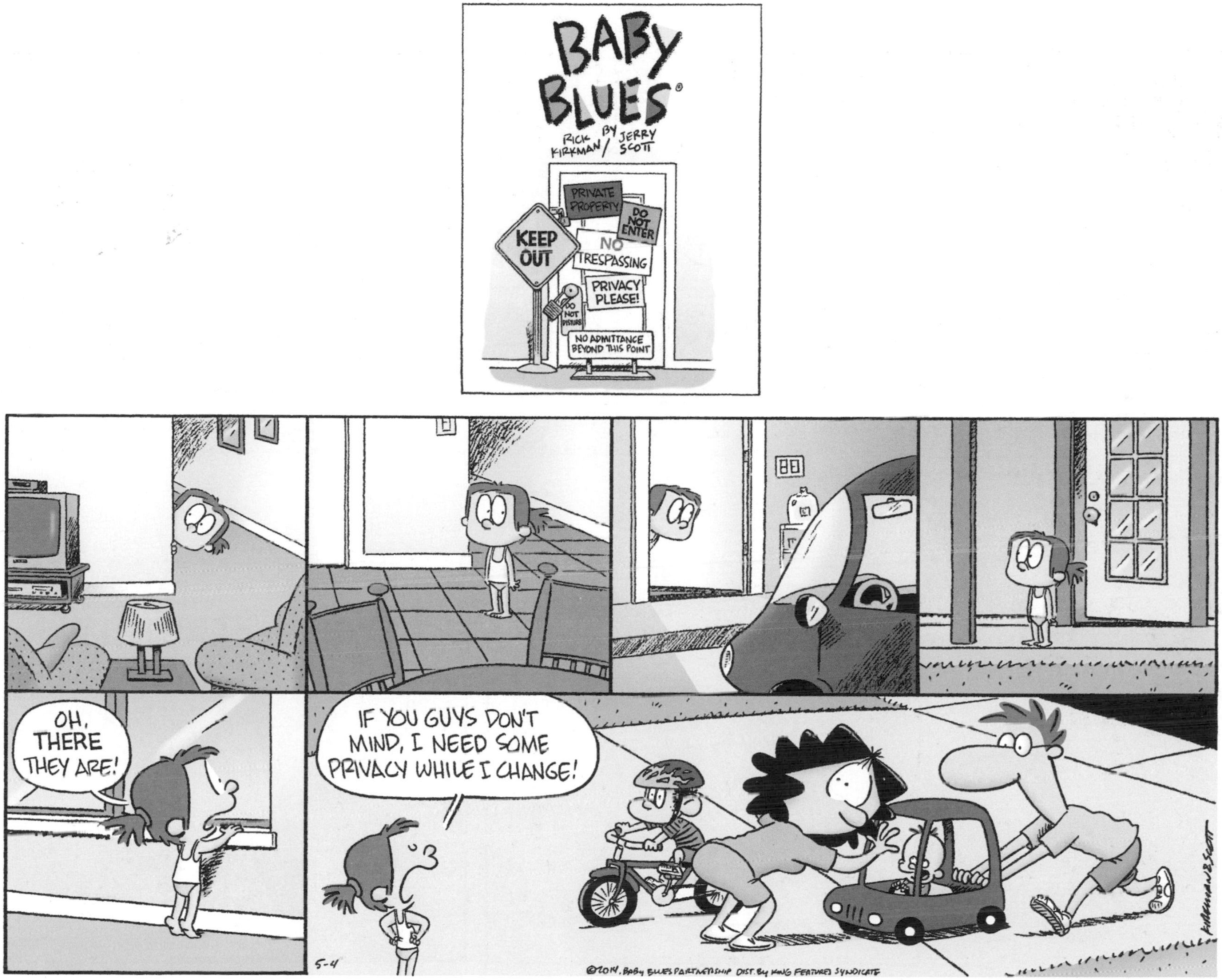
BABY BLUES®
BY RICK KIRKMAN / JERRY SCOTT
PRIVATE PROPERTY
DO NOT ENTER
KEEP OUT
NO TRESPASSING
PRIVACY PLEASE!
DO NOT DISTURB
NO ADMITTANCE BEYOND THIS POINT
OH, THERE THEY ARE!
IF YOU GUYS DON'T MIND, I NEED SOME PRIVACY WHILE I CHANGE!
KIRKMAN & SCOTT
5-4
©2014, BABY BLUES PARTNERSHIP DIST. BY KING FEATURES SYNDICATE

Rick: Kids are such literalists.

Jerry: The poor MacPherson kids will probably never get a real pet as long as we have fun making strips like this.

Rick: Learning that instills fear in most people—not in Hammie.

Jerry: One time I had to go to the grocery store at 6 a.m. on Mother's Day to get pancake mix or something. The scramble of desperate, unshaven dads snagging gift-like items off the shelves was hilarious and became a *Baby Blues* strip.

Jerry: Hammie is my own voice from the past.

Rick: Ah, welcome to the real world, Hammie.

Jerry: Darryl = me. That's the math of it.

Rick: A notable title panel in the fact that it's the only one I've ever scanned from life. I cut out all those letters from magazines.

Jerry: It's the peanut butter wedged into the spaces around the buttons that makes me crazy.

Rick: I don't know, I have to respect Hammie's ingenuity. And . . . owwwww.

Jerry: Coccyx somehow sounds less acceptable for the comics than "butt bone."

Rick: As they say: Don't try this at home.

Jerry: I don't make everything up. One time it really did take eight hours for my wife to trim our daughter's bangs.

Jerry: Try writing a comic strip with a six-year-old boy in it without including the occasional whizzing-in-the-flowers gag. Can't be done.

Jerry: When I was a kid, I figured out how to make our used riding mower pop a wheelie.
Mowing never looked so cool . . . or terrifying.

Rick: One of my favorite comebacks from Zoe.

Rick: This gag cracked me up. And the title panel did double-duty . . . see a few weeks later.

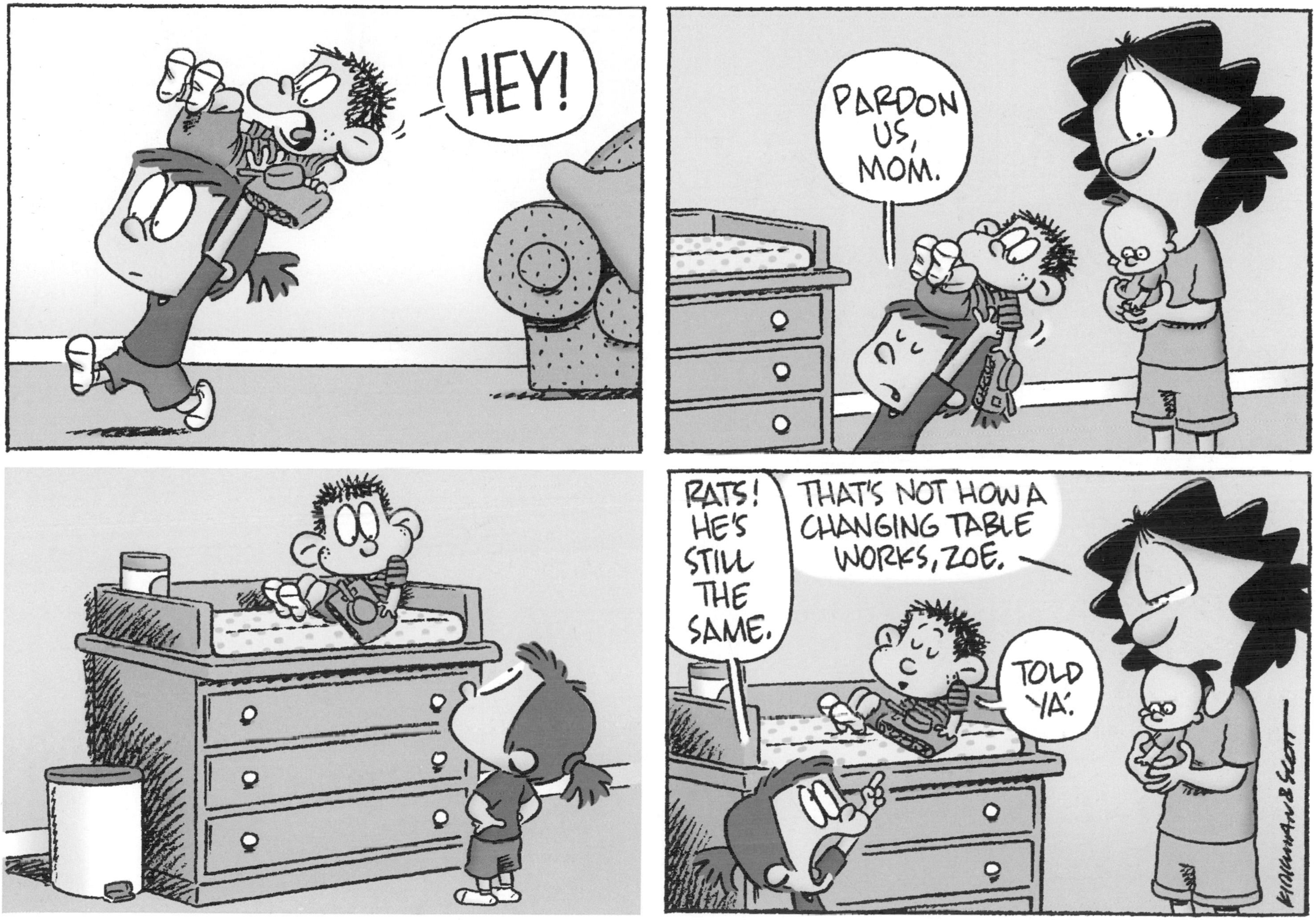
HEY!
PARDON US, MOM.
RATS! HE'S STILL THE SAME.
THAT'S NOT HOW A CHANGING TABLE WORKS, ZOE.
TOLD YA'.
KIRKMAN & SCOTT

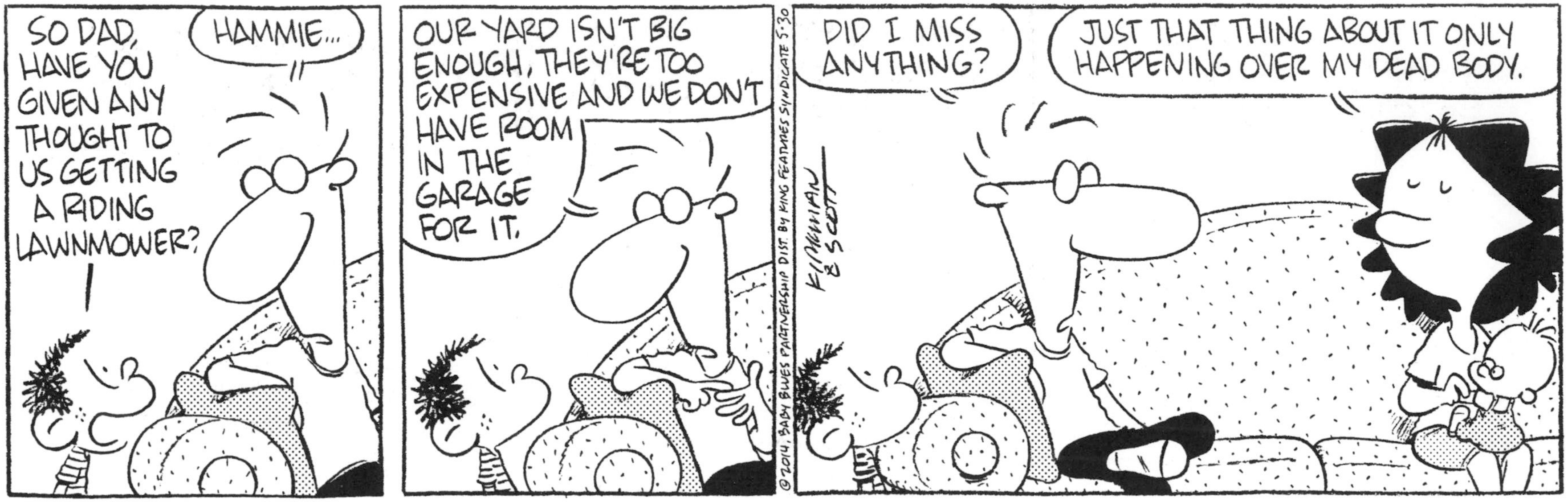
SO DAD, HAVE YOU GIVEN ANY THOUGHT TO US GETTING A RIDING LAWNMOWER?
HAMMIE...
OUR YARD ISN'T BIG ENOUGH, THEY'RE TOO EXPENSIVE AND WE DON'T HAVE ROOM IN THE GARAGE FOR IT.
©2014, BABY BLUES PARTNERSHIP DIST. BY KING FEATURES SYNDICATE 5-30
KIRKMAN & SCOTT
DID I MISS ANYTHING?
JUST THAT THING ABOUT IT ONLY HAPPENING OVER MY DEAD BODY.

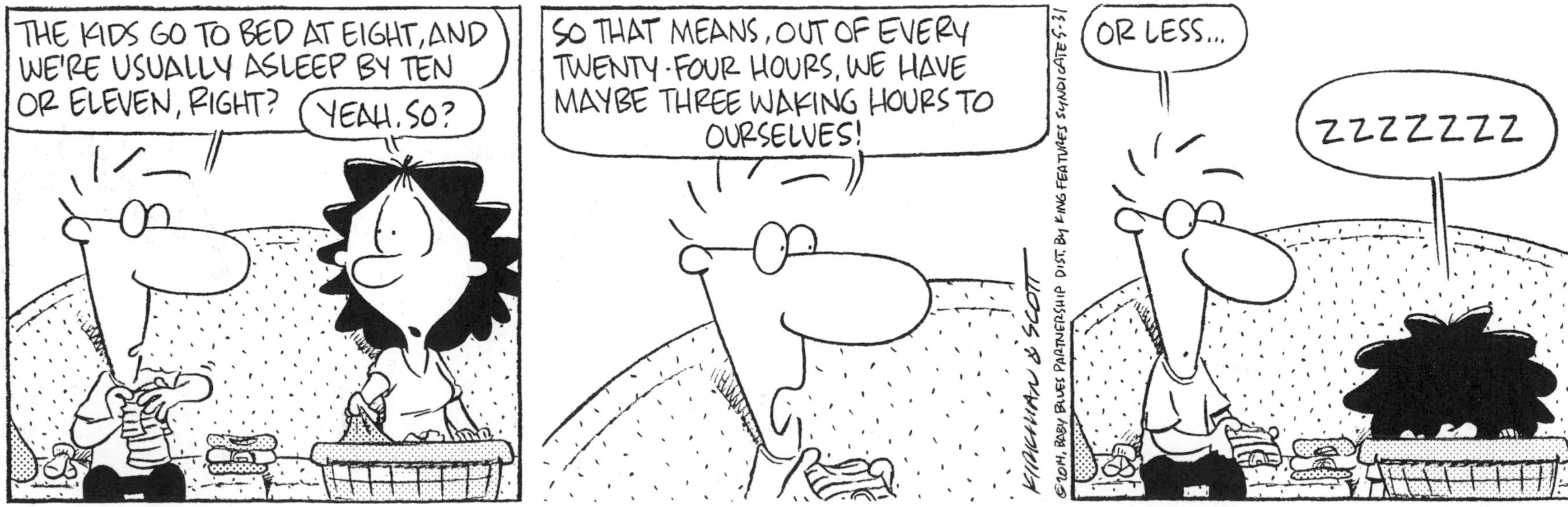
THE KIDS GO TO BED AT EIGHT, AND WE'RE USUALLY ASLEEP BY TEN OR ELEVEN, RIGHT?
YEAH. SO?
SO THAT MEANS, OUT OF EVERY TWENTY-FOUR HOURS, WE HAVE MAYBE THREE WAKING HOURS TO OURSELVES!
KIRKMAN & SCOTT
©2014, BABY BLUES PARTNERSHIP DIST. BY KING FEATURES SYNDICATE 5-31
OR LESS...
ZZZZZZZ

Jerry: #27 is good, but #41 has brought underwear inspection to a whole new level.

Jerry: We should make *Baby Blues* emoticons. Wouldn't they be more fun than those creepy yellow circle-headed things?

Rick: Did he really say that out loud? Has he learned nothing?

Rick: The gag brought to mind the old song by The Band, "The Weight." It's a little tip o' the hat to the late Levon Helm, who sang it. Wanda as Levon from Woodstock in 1969.

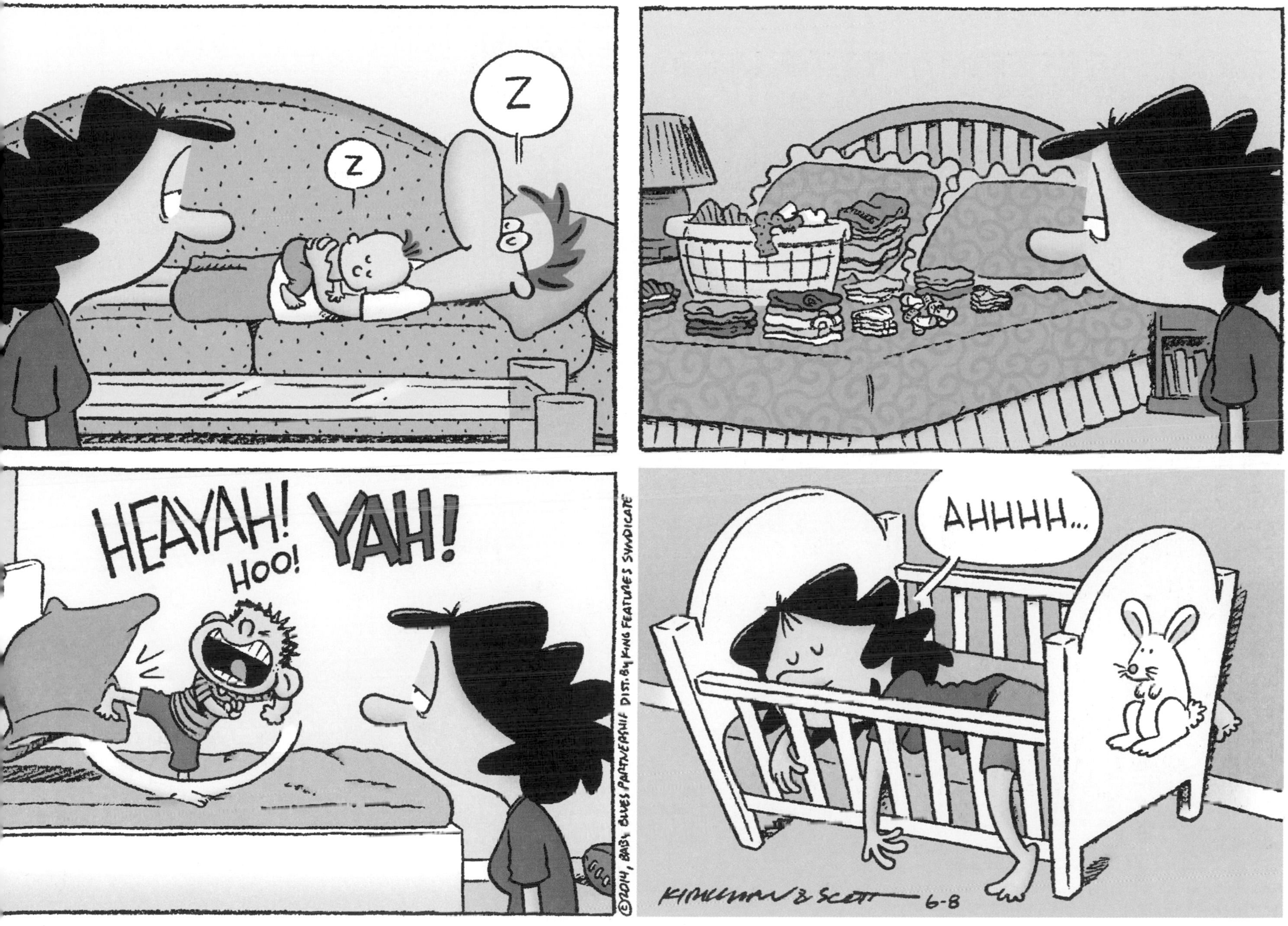
Z
Z
HEAYAH!
HOO!
YAH!
©2014, BABY BLUES PARTNERSHIP DIST. BY KING FEATURES SYNDICATE
AHHHH...
KIRKMAN & SCOTT 6-8

Rick: Coming up with one-time characters can be a minor challenge. It just happened that I'd seen this actual restaurant hostess a few days earlier.

Jerry: Trent is looking more menacing as he gets older. He's even making me nervous, and I invented him.

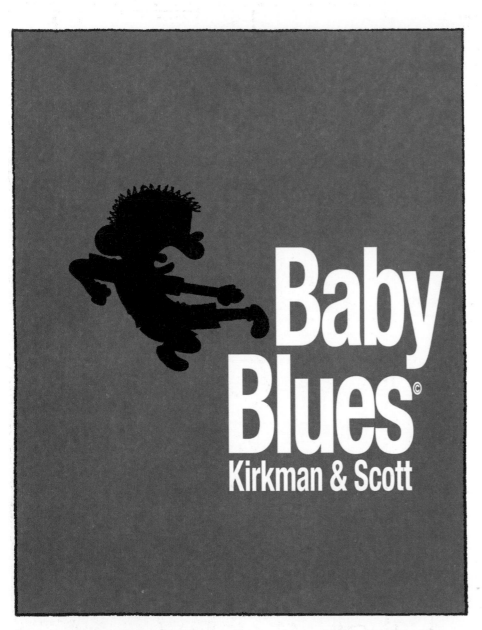

Baby Blues©
Kirkman & Scott

Jerry: Is every boy born with an overactive karate gene? More amazing action drawing by Rick!

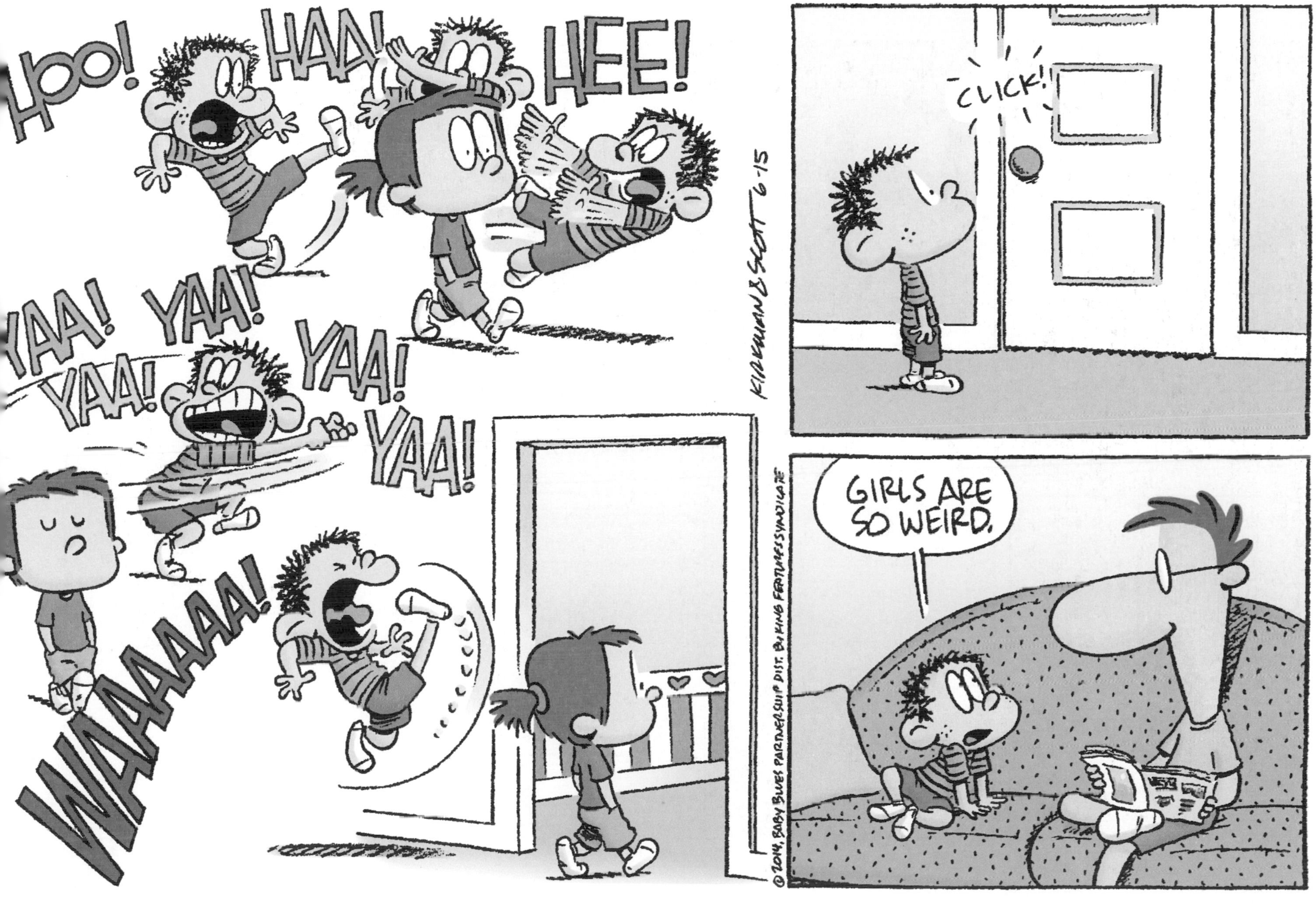
HOO!
HAA!
HEE!
YAA!
YAA!
YAA!
YAA!
YAA!
WAAAAAA!
KIRKMAN & SCOTT 6-15
CLICK!
GIRLS ARE SO WEIRD.
© 2014, BABY BLUES PARTNERSHIP DIST. BY KING FEATURES SYNDICATE

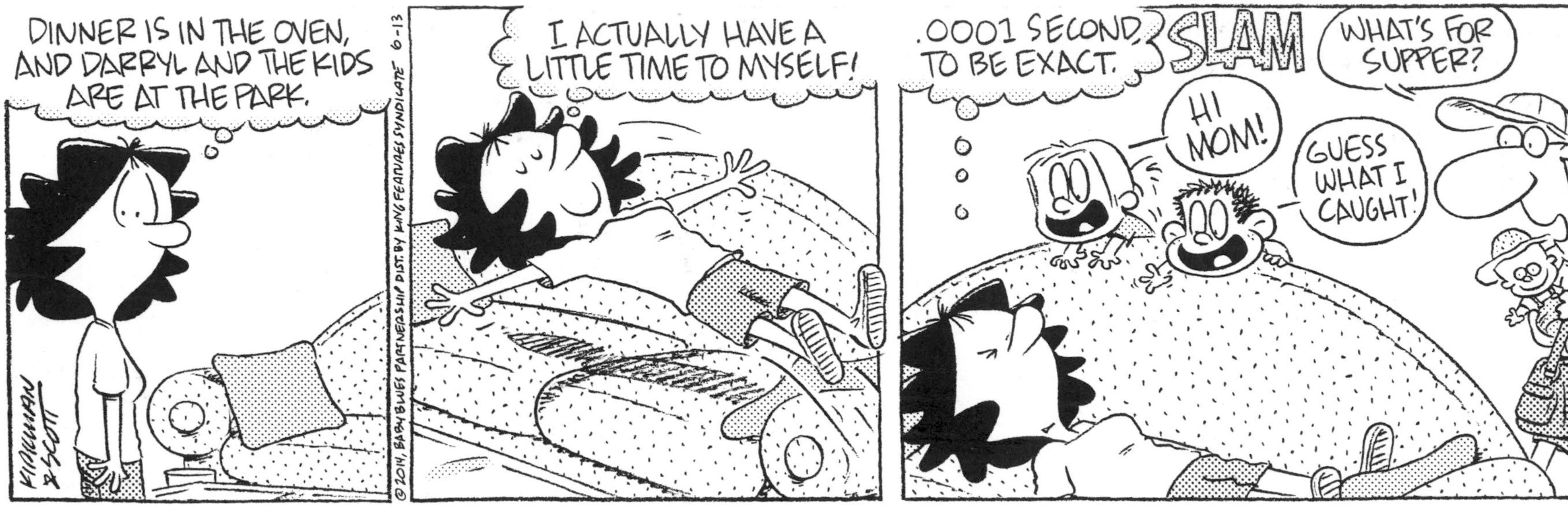
DINNER IS IN THE OVEN, AND DARRYL AND THE KIDS ARE AT THE PARK.
KIRKMAN & SCOTT
© 2014, BABY BLUES PARTNERSHIP DIST. BY KING FEATURES SYNDICATE 6-13
I ACTUALLY HAVE A LITTLE TIME TO MYSELF!
.0001 SECOND TO BE EXACT.
SLAM
WHAT'S FOR SUPPER?
HI MOM!
GUESS WHAT I CAUGHT!

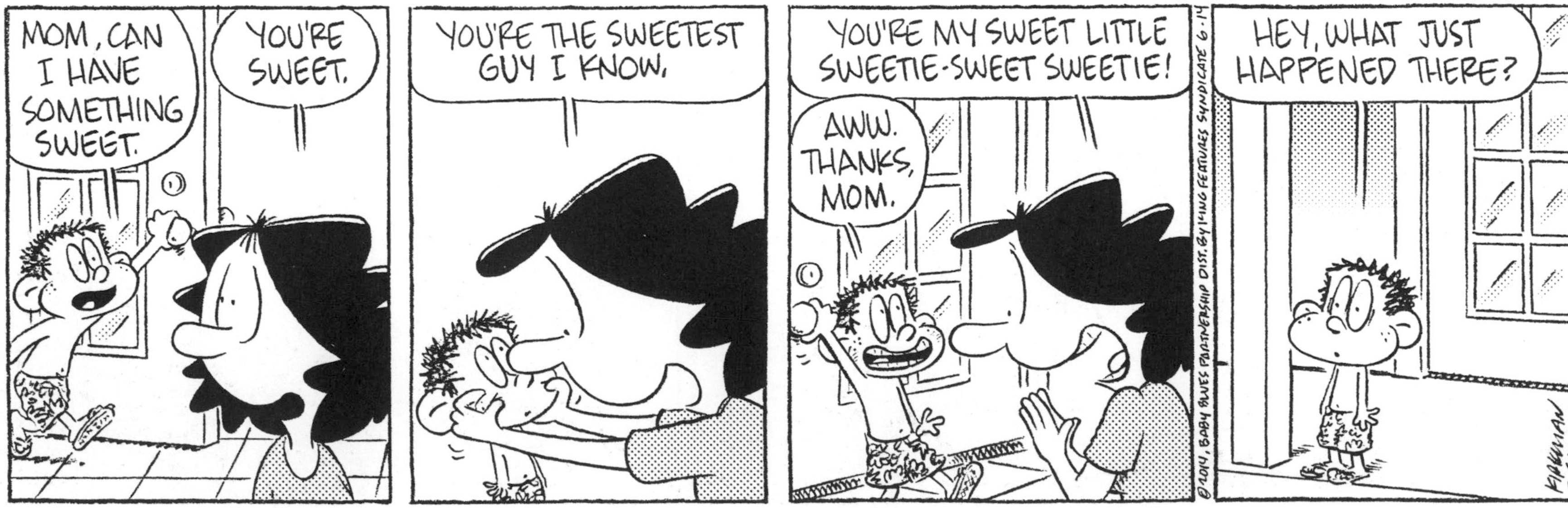
MOM, CAN I HAVE SOMETHING SWEET.
YOU'RE SWEET.
YOU'RE THE SWEETEST GUY I KNOW.
YOU'RE MY SWEET LITTLE SWEETIE-SWEET SWEETIE!
AWW. THANKS, MOM.
© 2014, BABY BLUES PARTNERSHIP DIST. BY KING FEATURES SYNDICATE 6-14
HEY, WHAT JUST HAPPENED THERE?
KIRKMAN & SCOTT

Rick: In my Little League days, I remember one team I was on went the whole season without a win. Surprisingly, we were named the Cubs.

Jerry: I played on a Little League team the summer between fifth and sixth grade. I never got a hit and only got to first base once when a pitch hit me in the back. The opposing teams loved me.

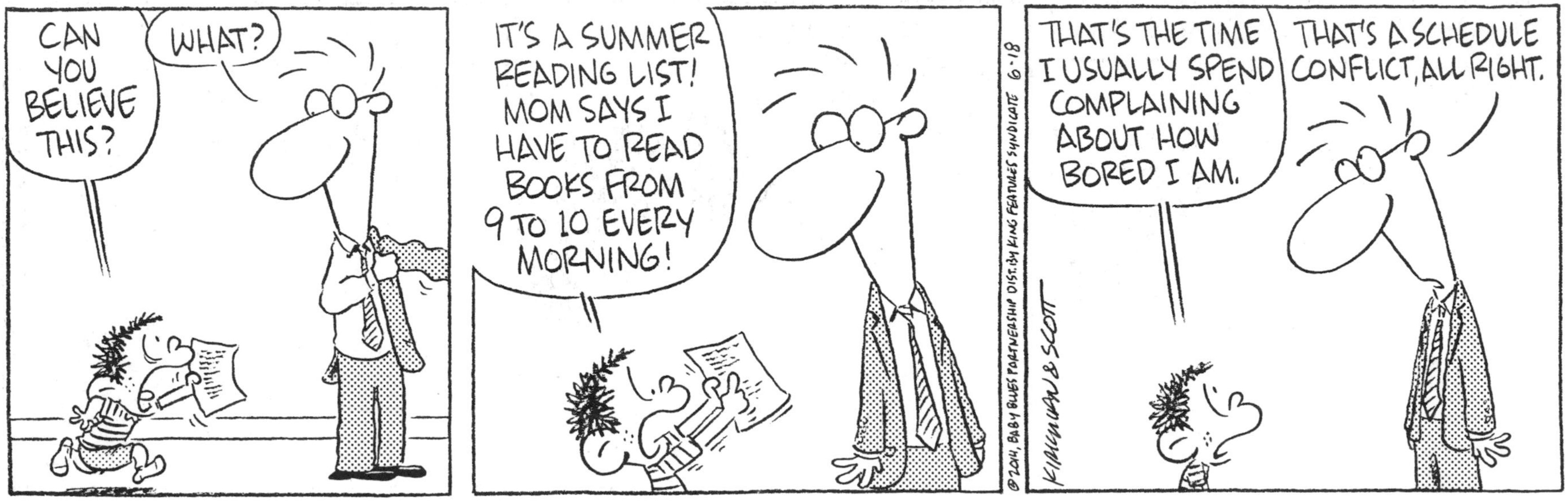
CAN YOU BELIEVE THIS?
WHAT?
IT'S A SUMMER READING LIST! MOM SAYS I HAVE TO READ BOOKS FROM 9 TO 10 EVERY MORNING!
© 2014, BABY BLUES PARTNERSHIP DIST. BY KING FEATURES SYNDICATE 6-18
KIRKMAN & SCOTT
THAT'S THE TIME I USUALLY SPEND COMPLAINING ABOUT HOW BORED I AM.
THAT'S A SCHEDULE CONFLICT, ALL RIGHT.

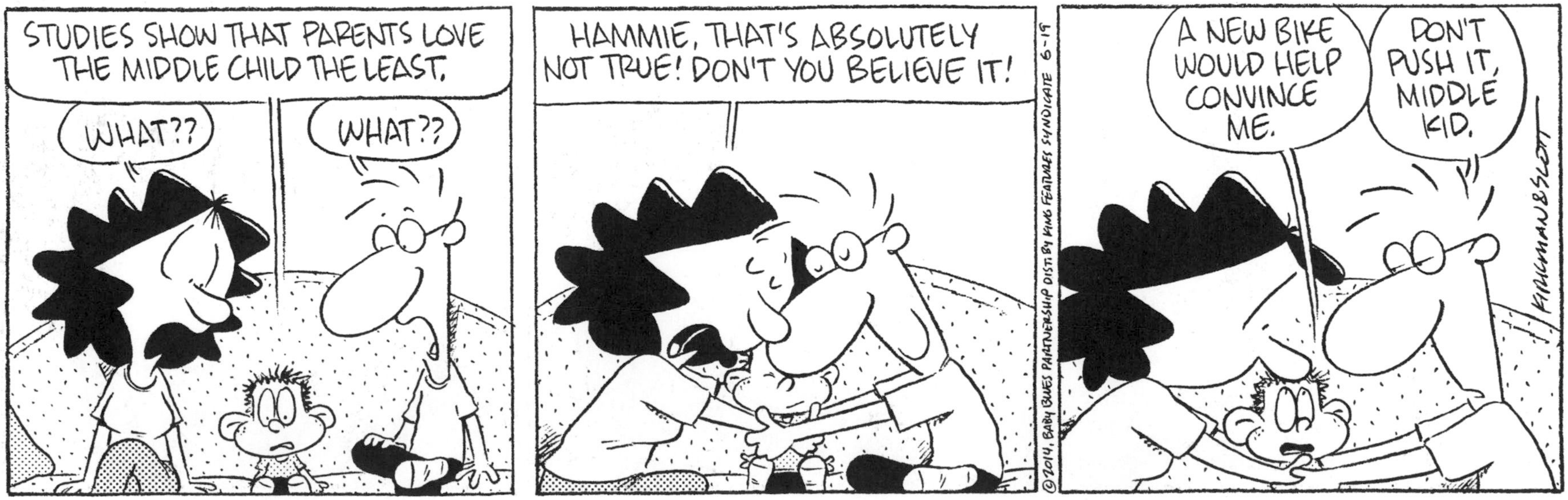
STUDIES SHOW THAT PARENTS LOVE THE MIDDLE CHILD THE LEAST.
WHAT??
WHAT??
HAMMIE, THAT'S ABSOLUTELY NOT TRUE! DON'T YOU BELIEVE IT!
© 2014, BABY BLUES PARTNERSHIP DIST. BY KING FEATURES SYNDICATE 6-19
A NEW BIKE WOULD HELP CONVINCE ME.
DON'T PUSH IT, MIDDLE KID.
KIRKMAN & SCOTT

Rick: I love Hammie's suspiciousness of Zoe.

Jerry: This strip was a shoutout to my pal, Leigh Rubin, who does the comic panel, *Rubes*. For the record, Leigh is neither loud nor odoriferous.

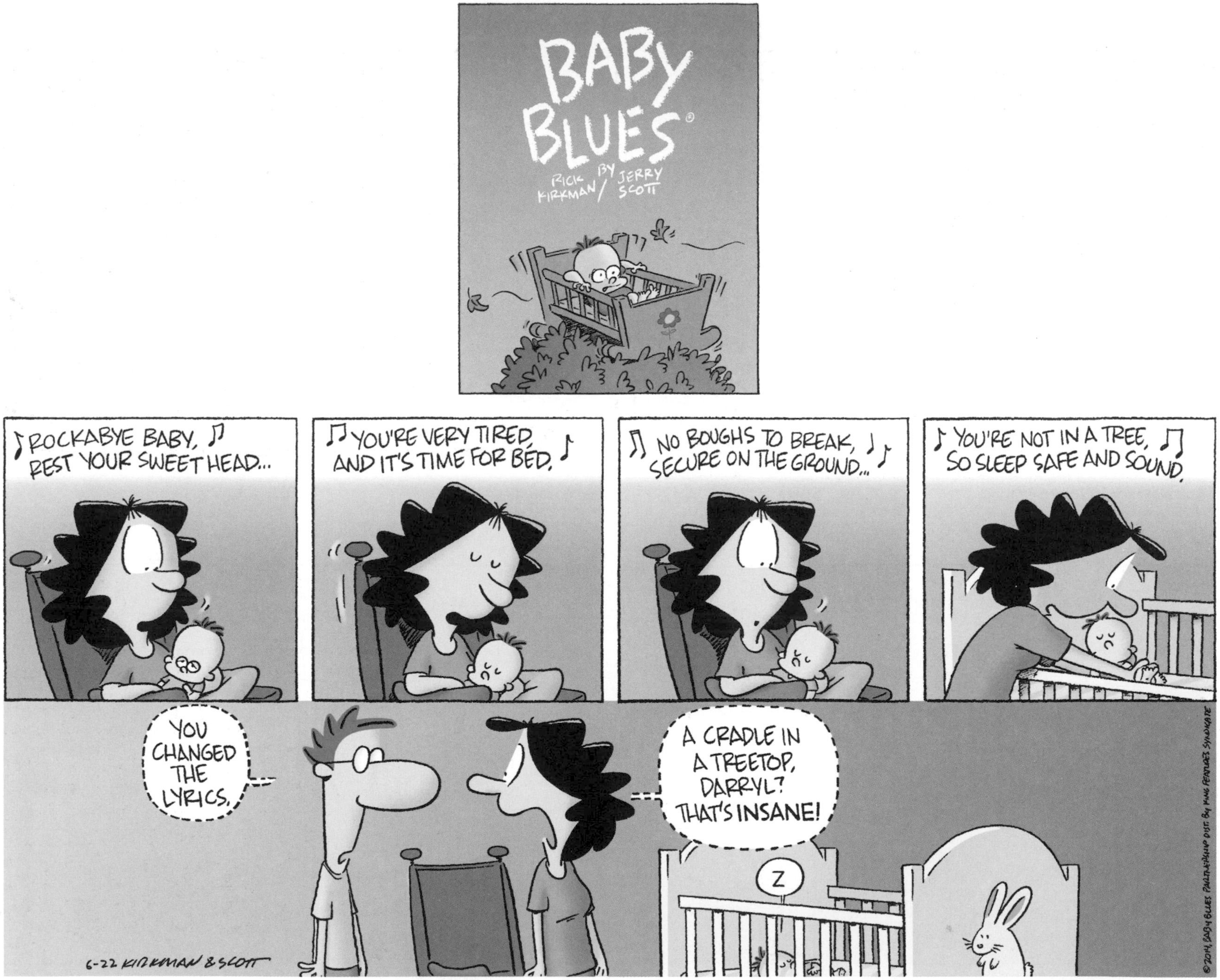
BABY BLUES®
BY RICK KIRKMAN / JERRY SCOTT
ROCKABYE BABY, REST YOUR SWEET HEAD...
YOU'RE VERY TIRED, AND IT'S TIME FOR BED.
NO BOUGHS TO BREAK, SECURE ON THE GROUND...
YOU'RE NOT IN A TREE, SO SLEEP SAFE AND SOUND.
YOU CHANGED THE LYRICS.
A CRADLE IN A TREETOP, DARRYL? THAT'S INSANE!
Z
6-22 KIRKMAN & SCOTT
© 2014 BABY BLUES PARTNERSHIP DIST. BY KING FEATURES SYNDICATE

Jerry: I have a few skills, but hair brushing/detangling isn't one of them. Somehow Darryl has the same issue.

Rick: If you look really closely, you can see that the aircraft carrier is the *USS Enterprise*. I spent some time on that ship with some cartoonists buddies and 5,500 of our closest military friends during a USO tour. The *Enterprise* was decommissioned soon after and now resides in the MacPherson bathtub.

Rick: Flashback! Flashback!

Jerry: In our house we called this "The Handoff."

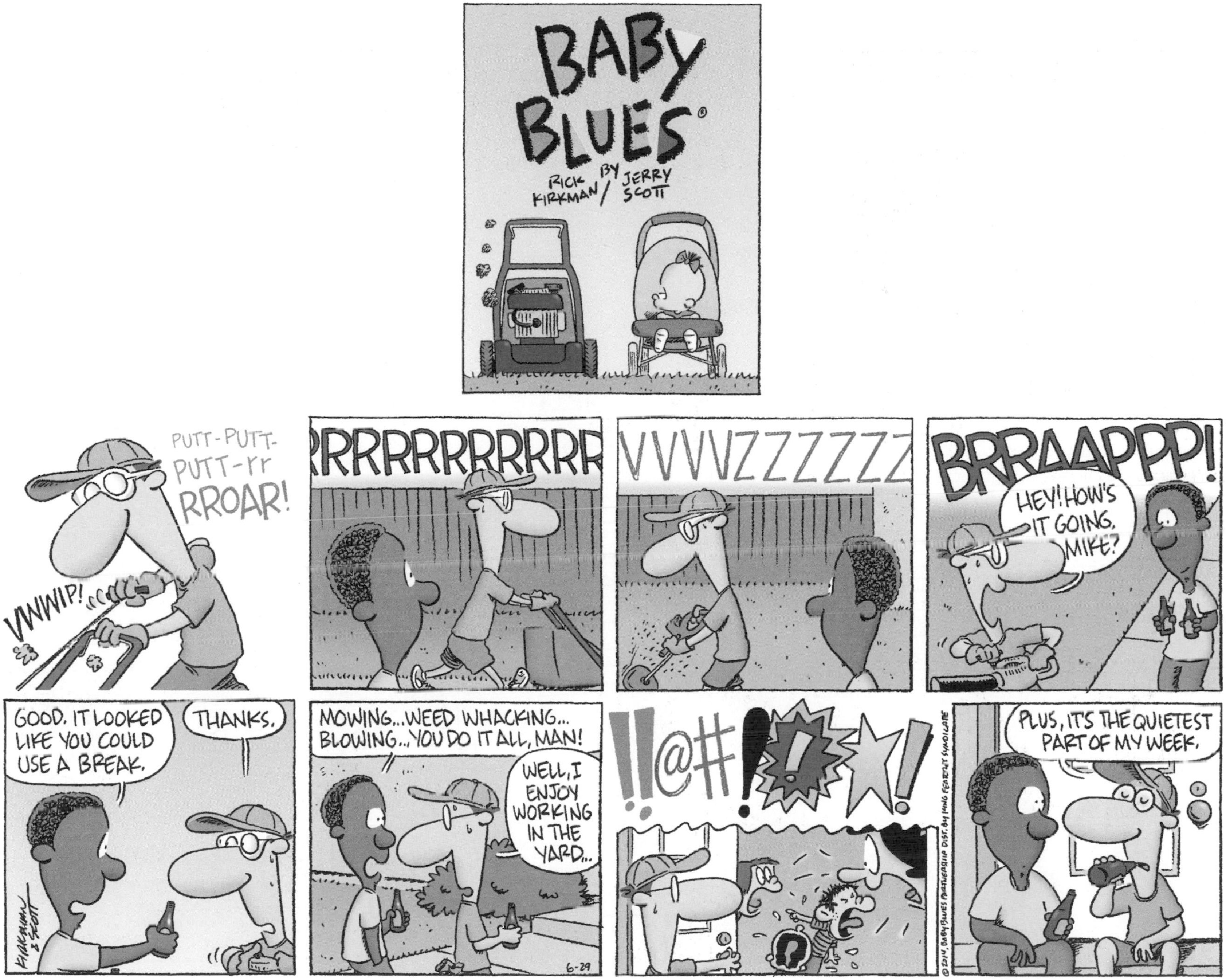
BABY BLUES®
BY RICK KIRKMAN / JERRY SCOTT
PUTT-PUTT-PUTT-rr RROAR!
VWWIP!
RRRRRRRRRRRR
VVVVZZZZZZ
BRRAAPPP!
HEY! HOW'S IT GOING, MIKE?
GOOD. IT LOOKED LIKE YOU COULD USE A BREAK.
THANKS.
KIRKMAN & SCOTT
MOWING... WEED WHACKING... BLOWING... YOU DO IT ALL, MAN!
WELL, I ENJOY WORKING IN THE YARD...
6-29
!!@#!!!
©2014, BABY BLUES PARTNERSHIP DIST. BY KING FEATURES SYNDICATE
PLUS, IT'S THE QUIETEST PART OF MY WEEK.

Rick: That line was told to me by someone whose kid said it. Too bad I can't remember who it was. Dang—I hate it when that happens. Thanks, whoever you are!

Jerry: The punchline in this strip came from one of my daughter's friends. She was describing the utter grossness of one of her brother's friends in her native kindergarten vocabulary.

Rick: The gag from Jerry read: "Zoe and Hammie are lounging around amid a ton of toys carelessly scattered around the living room." Let's play a game: How many things can you count scattered around panel 2?

Jerry: Mmmm . . . pudding scabs.

Rick: Some fun-to-draw action. Soccer balls drive me crazy, though.

Jerry: I hope grandmas never stop sending real letters, no matter how much it confuses the grandkids.

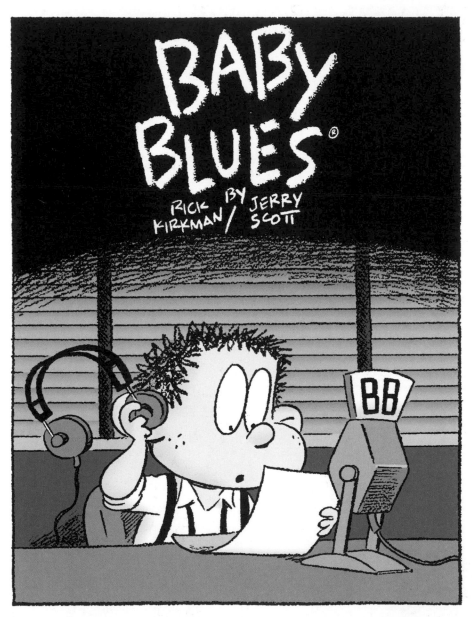

Rick: More title panel obsession: Here, Edward R. Murrow. Minus the cigarettes.

GOOD EVENING, LADIES AND GENTLEMEN, AND WELCOME TO MY INTERVIEW WITH ZOE MacPHERSON!

7-6

HE'S BRILLIANT, ATHLETIC, GOOD-LOOKING... THE LIST GOES ON.

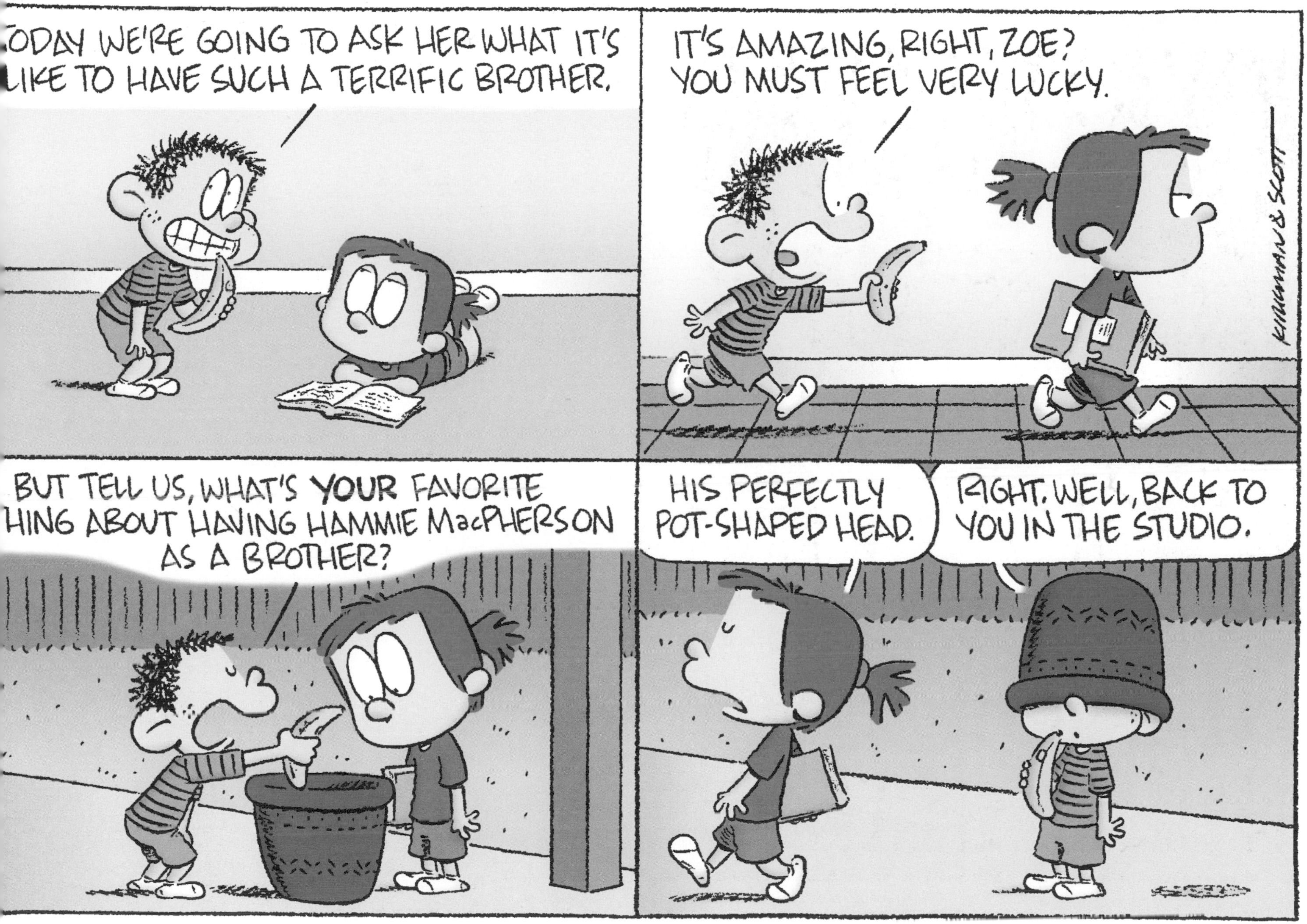
ODAY WE'RE GOING TO ASK HER WHAT IT'S LIKE TO HAVE SUCH A TERRIFIC BROTHER.
IT'S AMAZING, RIGHT, ZOE? YOU MUST FEEL VERY LUCKY.
KIRKMAN & SCOTT
BUT TELL US, WHAT'S **YOUR** FAVORITE HING ABOUT HAVING HAMMIE MacPHERSON AS A BROTHER?
HIS PERFECTLY POT-SHAPED HEAD.
RIGHT. WELL, BACK TO YOU IN THE STUDIO.

Rick: Sammie sketches exploring a different hairstyle before going back to the original title panel version.

Rick: This series with Sammie came from a Sunday title panel, where I drew various things with Hammie's head on them: A troll doll, a monkey, a goat, the man-eating plant from *Little Shop of Horrors* . . . and a little girl.

Rick: I really liked the look of the little girl with Hammie's face. After a couple weeks of staring at the drawing on my desk, I said to Jerry, "Wouldn't it be cool if Hammie met a girl who looked just like him?" And here's Sammie. Thanks, Jerry.

Rick: Love that middle panel. Just wish we could put scary music to it.

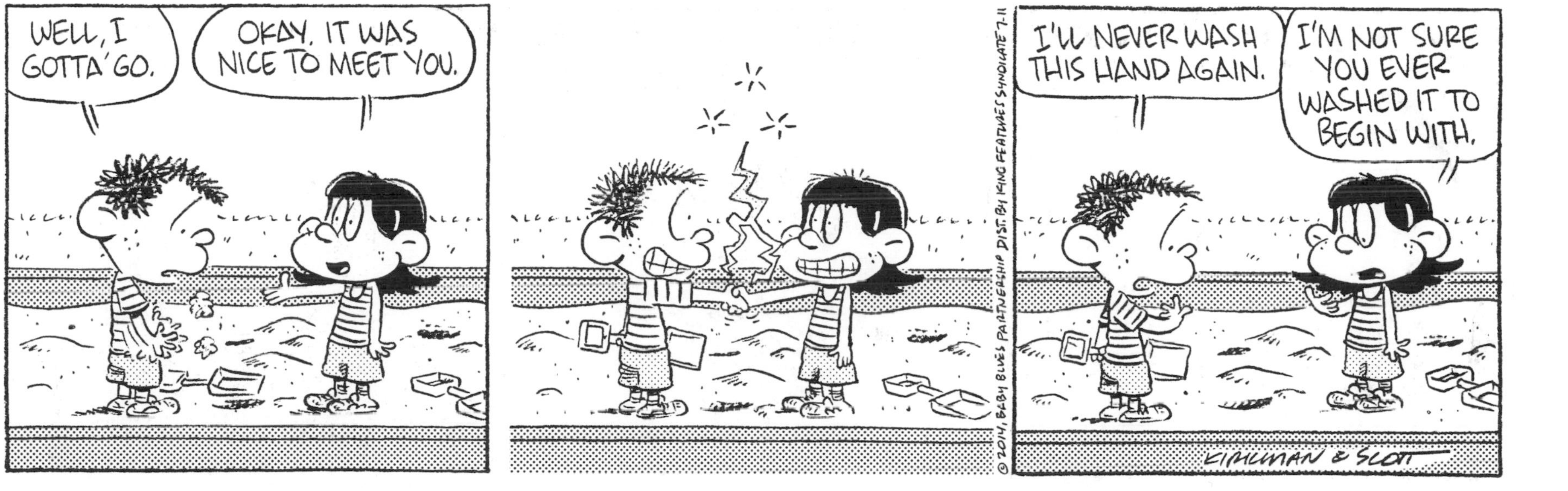
WELL, I GOTTA' GO.
OKAY. IT WAS NICE TO MEET YOU.
© 2014, BABY BLUES PARTNERSHIP DIST. BY KING FEATURES SYNDICATE 7-11
I'LL NEVER WASH THIS HAND AGAIN.
I'M NOT SURE YOU EVER WASHED IT TO BEGIN WITH.
KIRKMAN & SCOTT

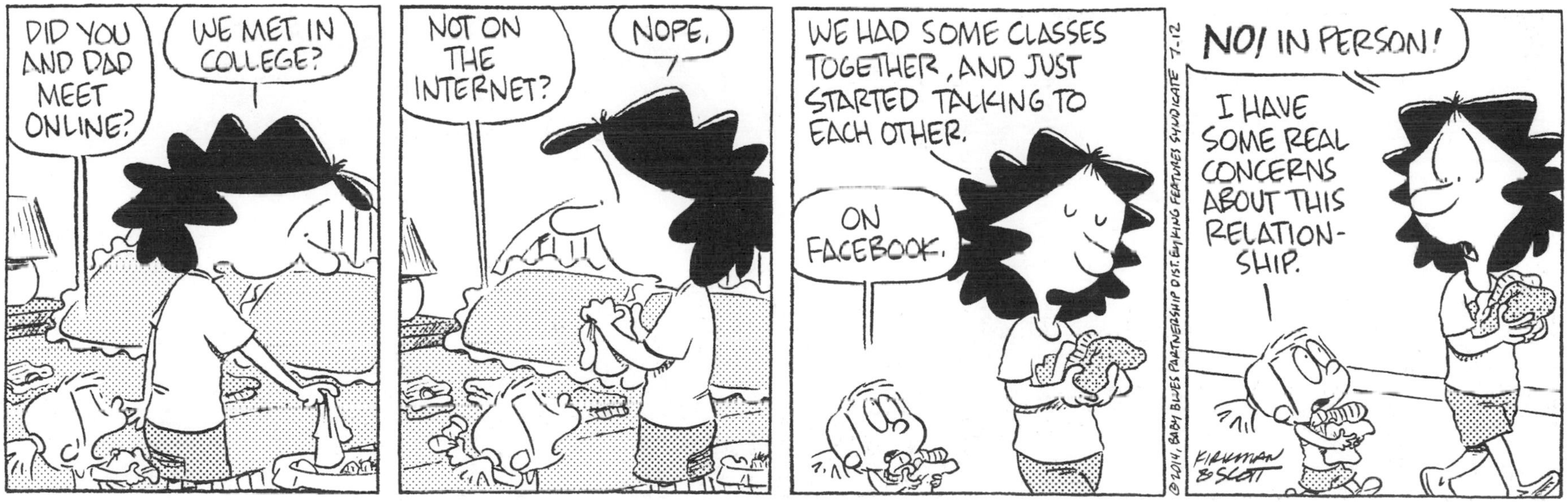
DID YOU AND DAD MEET ONLINE?
WE MET IN COLLEGE?
NOT ON THE INTERNET?
NOPE.
WE HAD SOME CLASSES TOGETHER, AND JUST STARTED TALKING TO EACH OTHER.
ON FACEBOOK.
© 2014, BABY BLUES PARTNERSHIP DIST. BY KING FEATURES SYNDICATE 7-12
NO! IN PERSON!
I HAVE SOME REAL CONCERNS ABOUT THIS RELATION-SHIP.
KIRKMAN & SCOTT

Jerry: This strip was ripped from real life. My daughter and her friends ended up camping in the living room that night with me on the couch as Bigfoot watchdog.

Jerry: Almost every parent knows when their kids talk back in their minds, but I don't think there was a word for it before this. You're welcome.

Jerry: Is there anything more satisfying than heckling a sibling?

Jerry: Am I the only one who thinks "cornhole" is a goofy name for a game that uses beanbags? Of course, "beanhole" would sound even goofier.

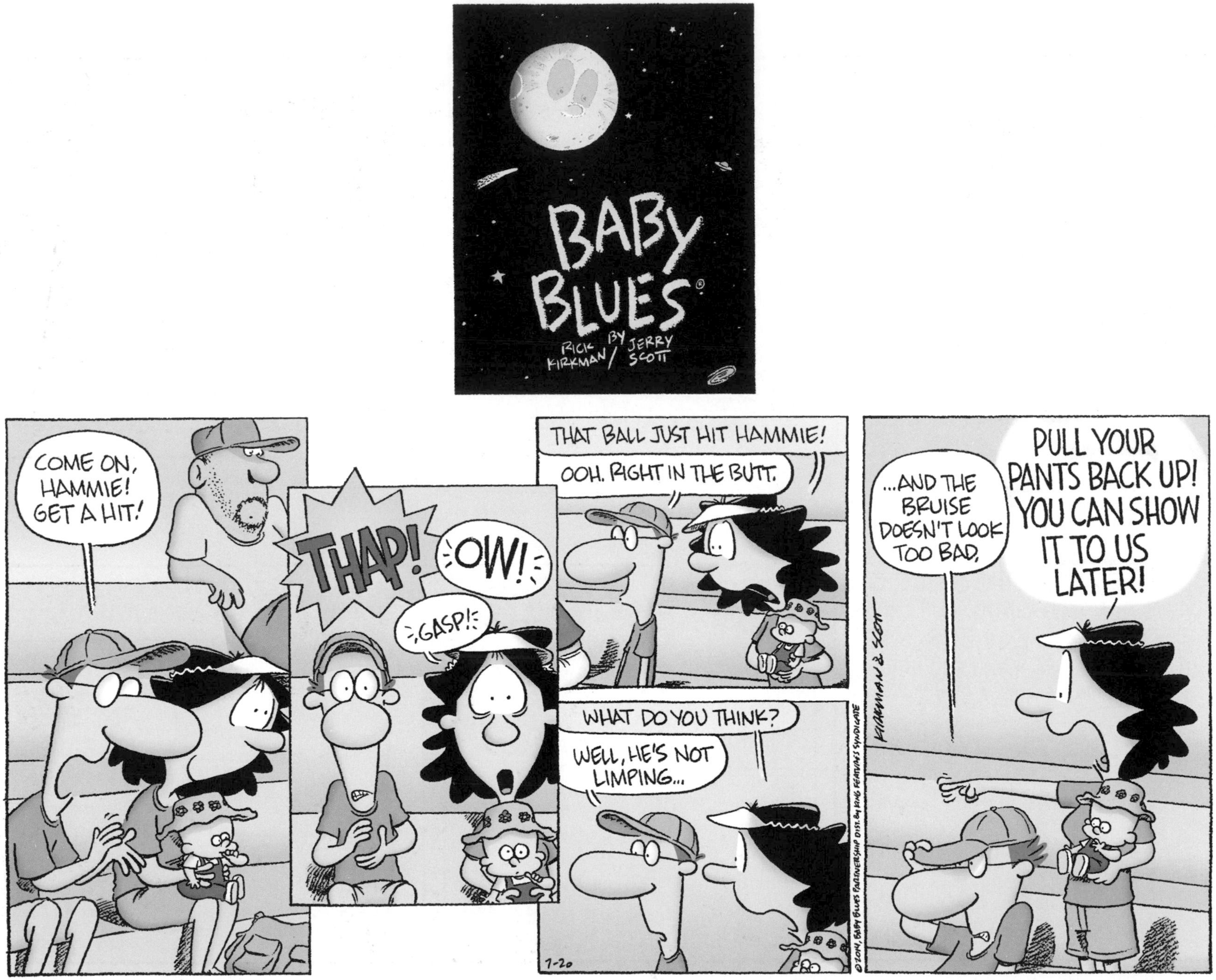
BABY BLUES®
BY RICK KIRKMAN / JERRY SCOTT
COME ON, HAMMIE! GET A HIT!
THAP!
OW!
GASP!
THAT BALL JUST HIT HAMMIE!
OOH. RIGHT IN THE BUTT.
WHAT DO YOU THINK?
WELL, HE'S NOT LIMPING...
7-20
© 2014, BABY BLUES PARTNERSHIP DIST. BY KING FEATURES SYNDICATE
KIRKMAN & SCOTT
...AND THE BRUISE DOESN'T LOOK TOO BAD.
PULL YOUR PANTS BACK UP! YOU CAN SHOW IT TO US LATER!

Jerry: This strip got some meaningful nods from readers. And by "readers" I mean "moms."

Rick: Technology giveth, and technology taketh away.

Jerry: If you don't have grass stains in your ears, you're not playing hard enough.

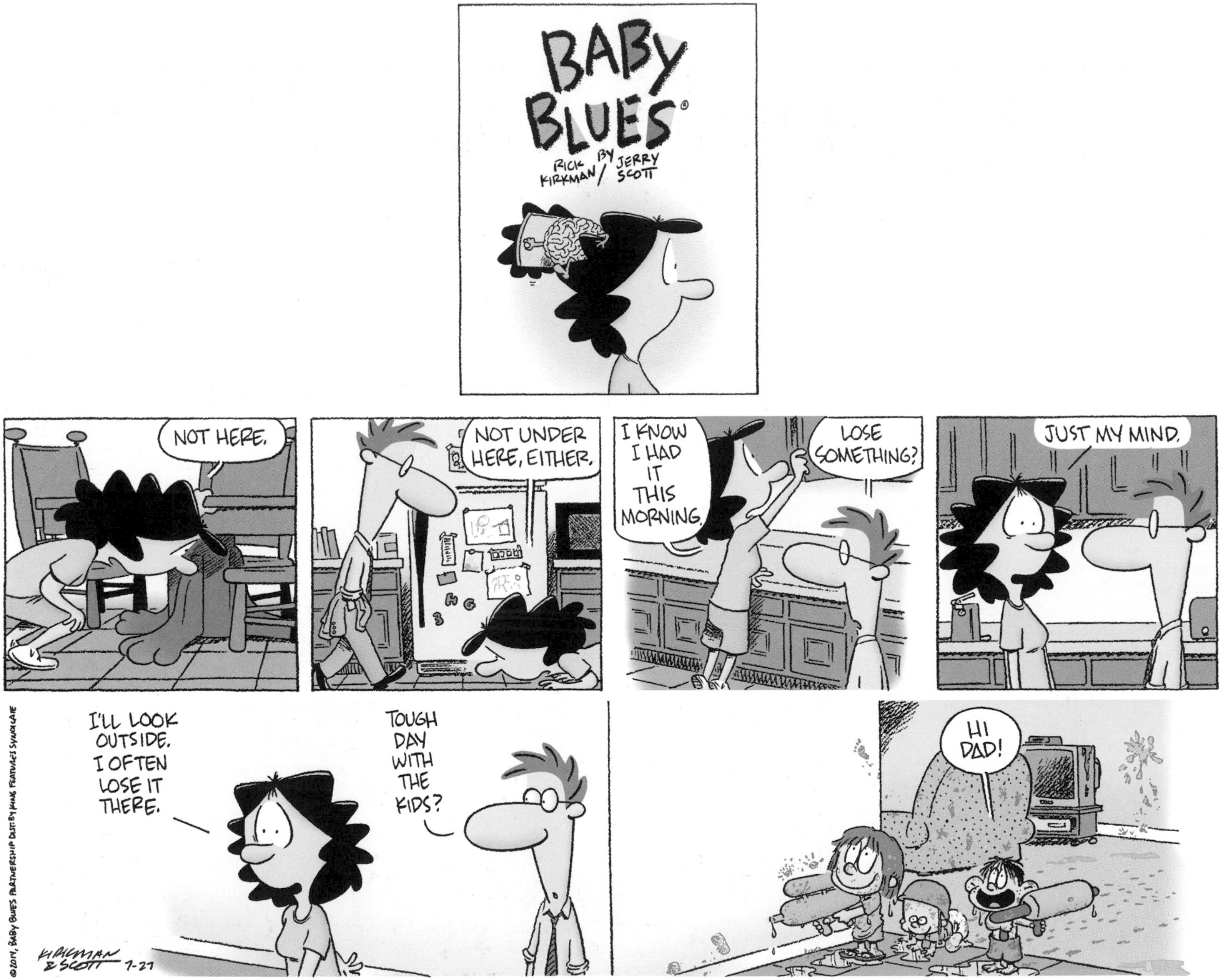
BABY BLUES®
BY RICK KIRKMAN / JERRY SCOTT
NOT HERE.
NOT UNDER HERE, EITHER.
I KNOW I HAD IT THIS MORNING.
LOSE SOMETHING?
JUST MY MIND.
I'LL LOOK OUTSIDE. I OFTEN LOSE IT THERE.
TOUGH DAY WITH THE KIDS?
HI DAD!
KIRKMAN & SCOTT 7-27
©2014, BABY BLUES PARTNERSHIP DIST. BY KING FEATURES SYNDICATE

Jerry: I was in charge of trophies for my daughter's soccer team when she was very young. Every kid got a trophy that year, and each one had to be engraved with the player's major attribute. I was going to name my kid "Best Snacker," but I got overruled.

Jerry: Every once in a while there's a strip idea that just needs to be drawn sideways.

Jerry: One of the cool things about comic strips is that you can write weird stuff like this.

Rick: Title panel obsession returns with my love of hand lettering and a fun transformation of Hammie into the Mighty Casey. Above are a few of the title panel sketches and the line art prior to coloring. Love the gag, too.

Rick: Hmm. I'm beginning to wonder how many things Jerry peed in when he was a kid.

Jerry: Can I see a show of hands from everyone who would like to see Rick draw a five-seater motorcycle?

Rick: Very funny, Jerry.

Rick: I definitely would've watched *Space Maggots* when I was a kid. For the record, this strip marks the day of Wren's hair growth spurt. She more than doubled her three hairs since her last appearance. I figured, if she's walking now, her hair should make more progress, too.

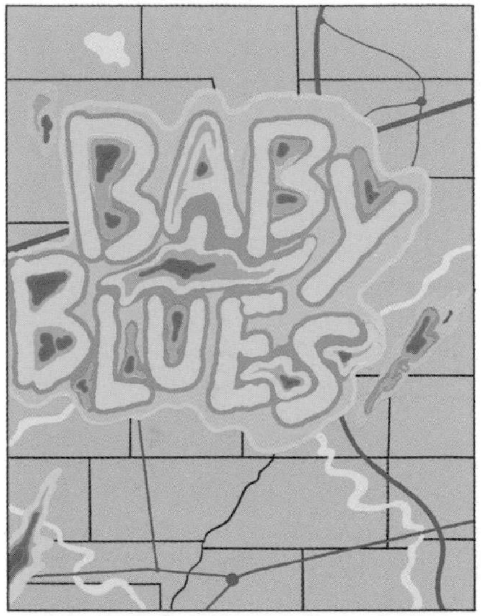
BABY BLUES

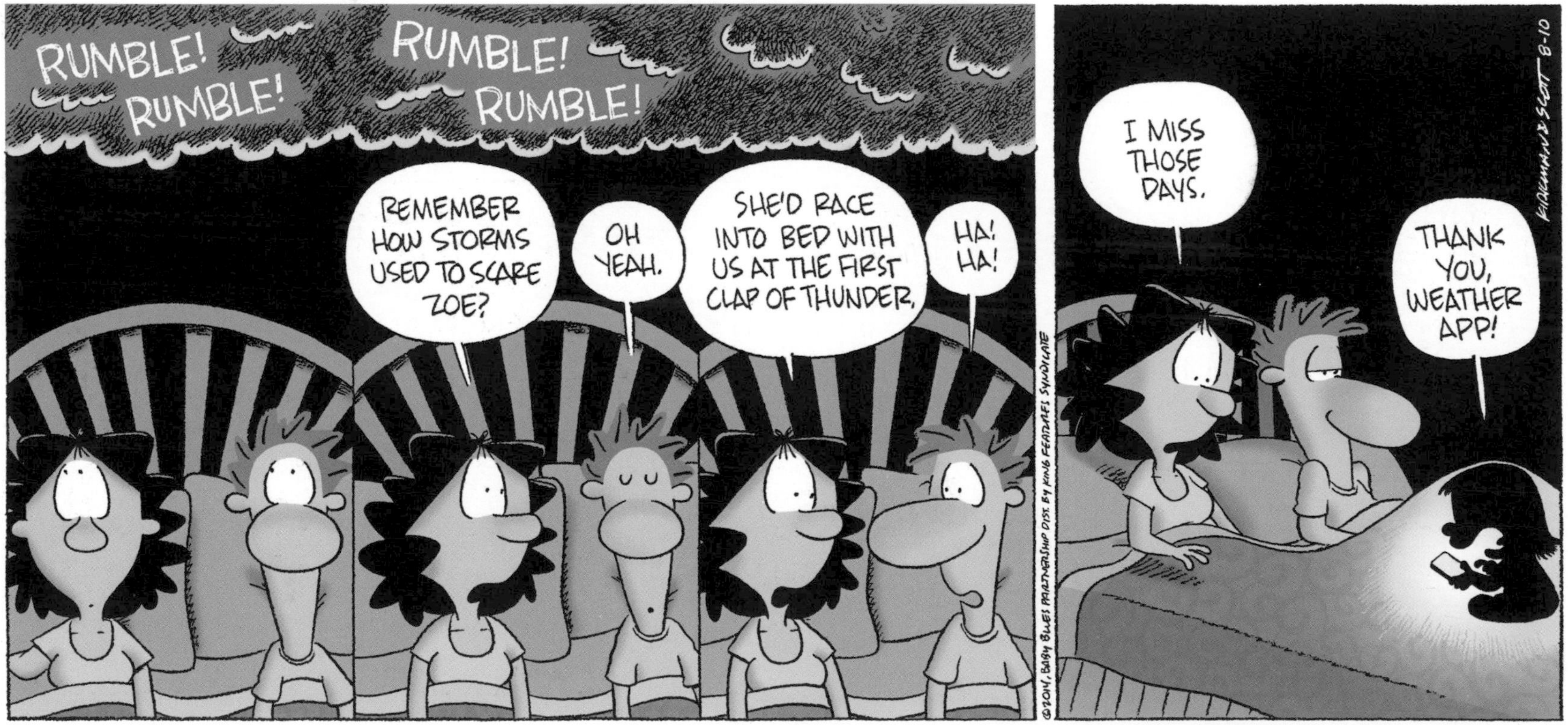
RUMBLE! RUMBLE!
RUMBLE! RUMBLE!
REMEMBER HOW STORMS USED TO SCARE ZOE?
OH YEAH.
SHE'D RACE INTO BED WITH US AT THE FIRST CLAP OF THUNDER.
HA! HA!
©2014, BABY BLUES PARTNERSHIP DIST. BY KING FEATURES SYNDICATE
KIRKMAN & SCOTT 8-10
I MISS THOSE DAYS.
THANK YOU, WEATHER APP!

Jerry: I can't believe Hammie forgot to draw the fangs. Guys always draw fangs.

Rick: Oh, the humiliation of being smoked by your kids at video games.

Jerry: Hammie's friend, Trent, has become synonymous with mayhem in *Baby Blues*. My apologies to all the non-ornery Trents out there.

Rick: Man, he walked into that one.

Jerry: I mentioned earlier that I wasn't good at things like brushing hair. Add using cling wrap to that list.

Rick: "Parkes" refers to a cartoonist friend, who coincidentally draws for a lot of board game boxes. I would love to see him sing that.

Jerry: This pretty much sums up the backyard sports at my house.

Rick: Yes, that's a Spaceman Spiff toy Hammie is playing with. Somebody had to make one, even if it's fictional.

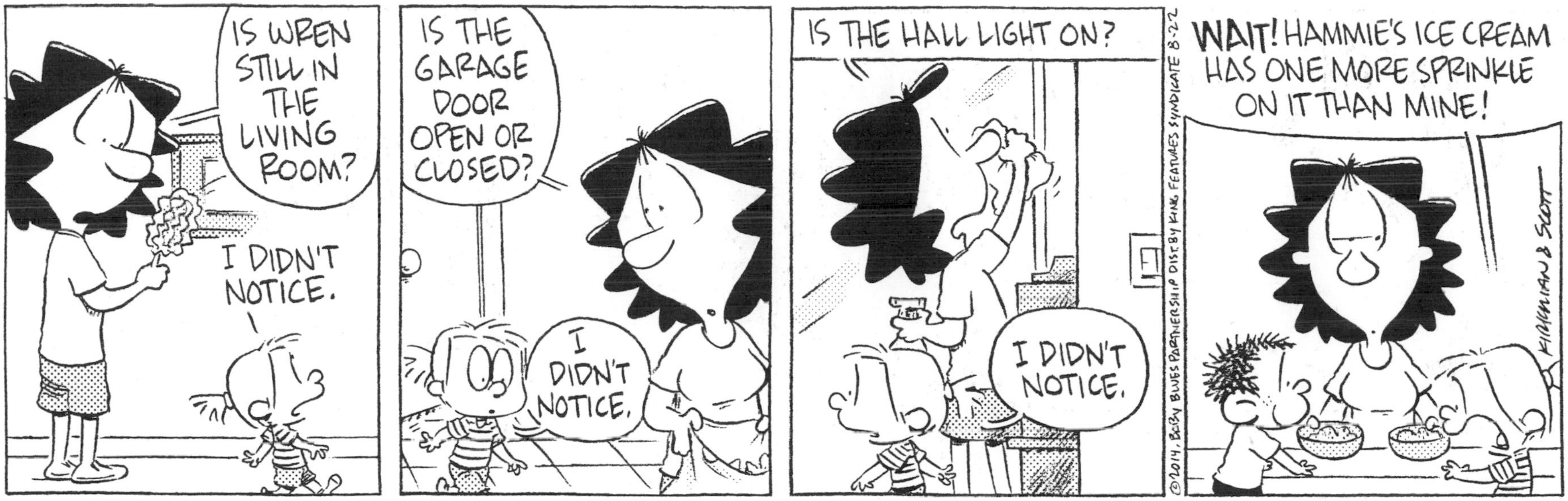
IS WREN STILL IN THE LIVING ROOM?
I DIDN'T NOTICE.
IS THE GARAGE DOOR OPEN OR CLOSED?
I DIDN'T NOTICE.
IS THE HALL LIGHT ON?
I DIDN'T NOTICE.
©2014, BABY BLUES PARTNERSHIP DIST BY KING FEATURES SYNDICATE 8-22
WAIT! HAMMIE'S ICE CREAM HAS ONE MORE SPRINKLE ON IT THAN MINE!
KIRKMAN & SCOTT

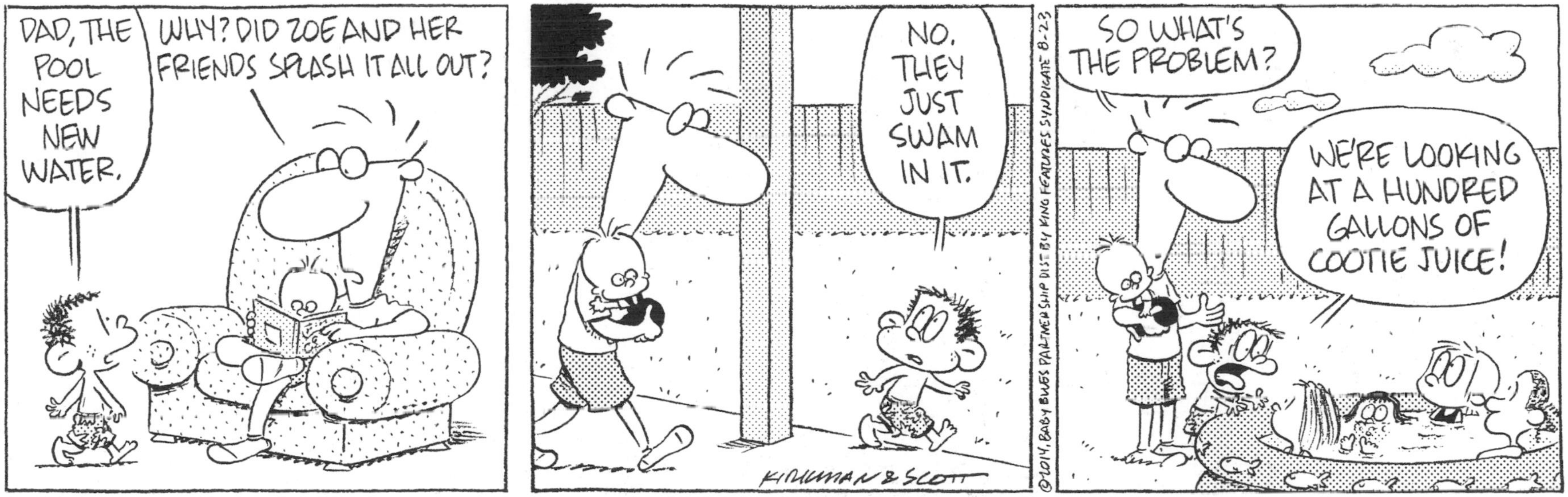
DAD, THE POOL NEEDS NEW WATER.
WHY? DID ZOE AND HER FRIENDS SPLASH IT ALL OUT?
NO. THEY JUST SWAM IN IT.
KIRKMAN & SCOTT
©2014, BABY BLUES PARTNERSHIP DIST BY KING FEATURES SYNDICATE 8-23
SO WHAT'S THE PROBLEM?
WE'RE LOOKING AT A HUNDRED GALLONS OF COOTIE JUICE!

Rick: This strip generated a lot of helpful teething hints in Facebook comments—along with a sad-face emoji with this comment: "How childishly behaving parents." Oh, well.

Jerry: Didn't Darryl lose his car keys back on February 25th, too?

Jerry: Some of my favorite strips to write are the ones where Hammie and Zoe are in complete opposition on any given subject. True or not, it's the way I remember growing up with my sisters . . . and we liked it that way.

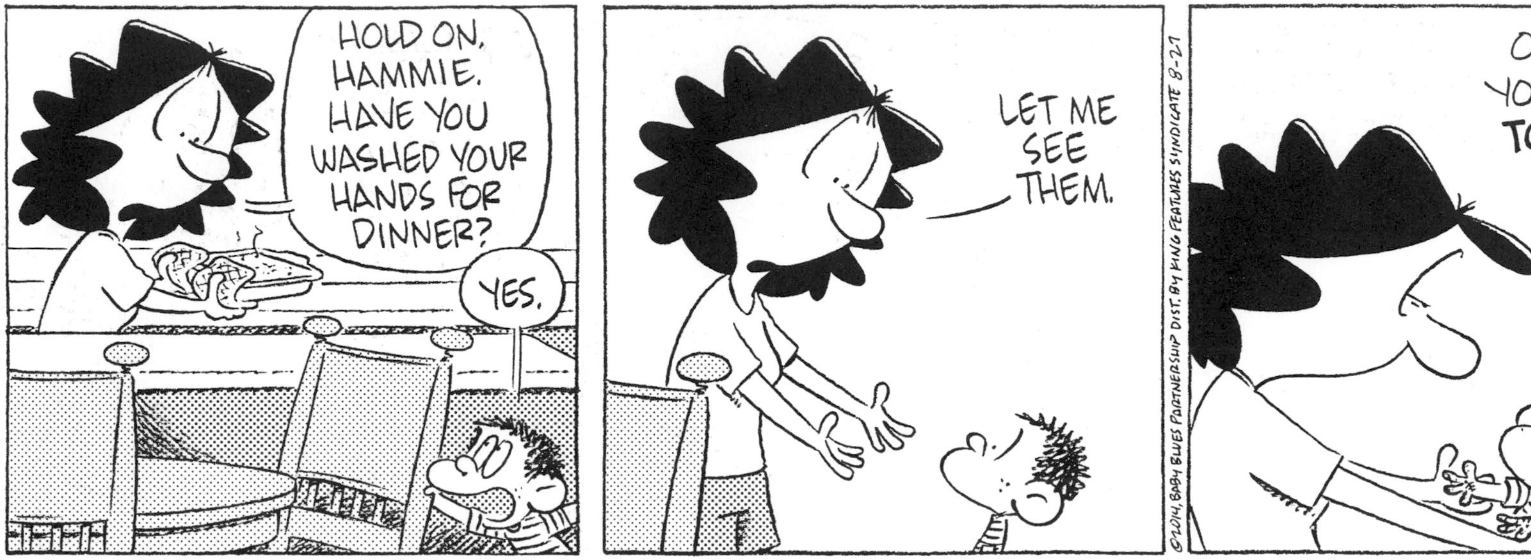
HOLD ON, HAMMIE. HAVE YOU WASHED YOUR HANDS FOR DINNER?
YES.
LET ME SEE THEM.
©2014, BABY BLUES PARTNERSHIP DIST. BY KING FEATURES SYNDICATE 8-27
OHHHH... YOU MEANT **TONIGHT'S** DINNER.
KIRKMAN & SCOTT

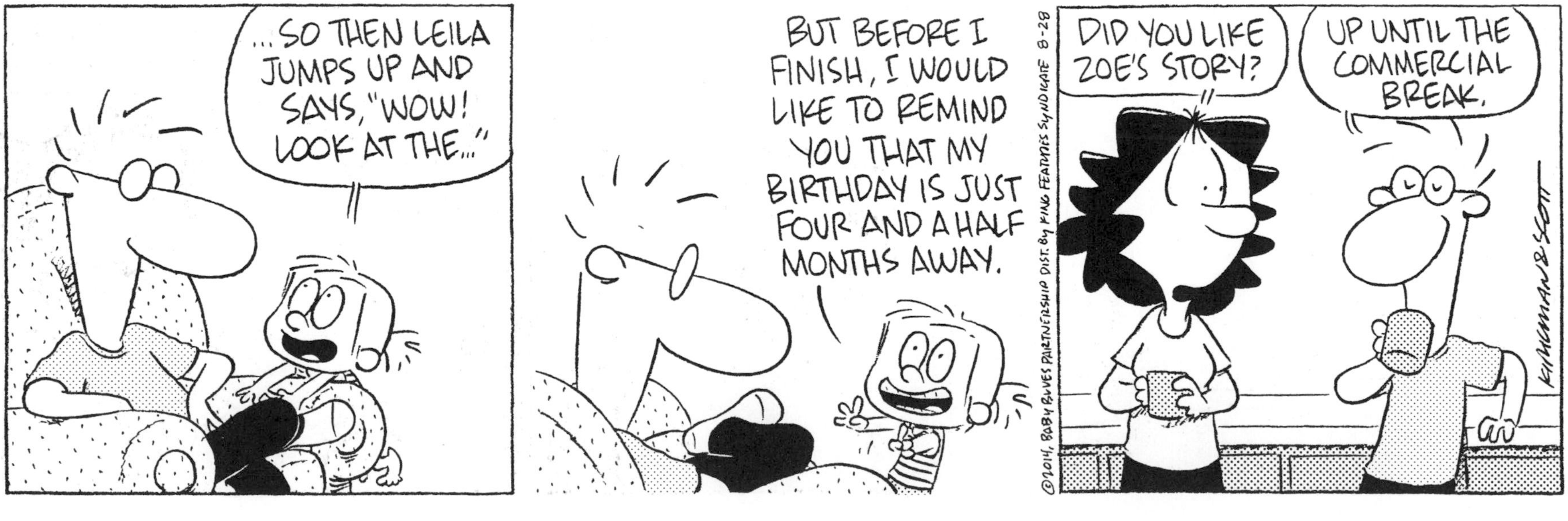
...SO THEN LEILA JUMPS UP AND SAYS, "WOW! LOOK AT THE..."
BUT BEFORE I FINISH, I WOULD LIKE TO REMIND YOU THAT MY BIRTHDAY IS JUST FOUR AND A HALF MONTHS AWAY.
©2014, BABY BLUES PARTNERSHIP DIST. BY KING FEATURES SYNDICATE 8-28
DID YOU LIKE ZOE'S STORY?
UP UNTIL THE COMMERCIAL BREAK.
KIRKMAN & SCOTT

Jerry: Every stage of a toddler's development is a new opportunity for friction.

Rick: Find the things in this panel Hammie has done to annoy his sisters. Hint: There are eight.

Jerry: One of our kids had a rocking horse and a pair of cowgirl boots. The rocking horse was her favorite toy, but the boots were the thing. She wore them to bed for like a month.

Rick: Ha! Great last line. If there was a Hammie version of the Bill of Rights, that would be written into it.

Rick: See previous strip.

Jerry: This looks like Hammie's been playing some version of One-Man Calvinball.

Rick: Ta-daa! Wren now has enough hair to cover the top of her head.

Rick: One of my favorite gags of the year—just a perfect answer.

Jerry: The Amazon drone in the title panel was totally Rick's idea, and it's a great one. Sometimes I think he should write and I should draw. Better yet, he could do both and I could take a few weeks off.

Rick: That was a load of fun to draw.

Jerry: Rick knocked it out of the park with the drawings in this strip!

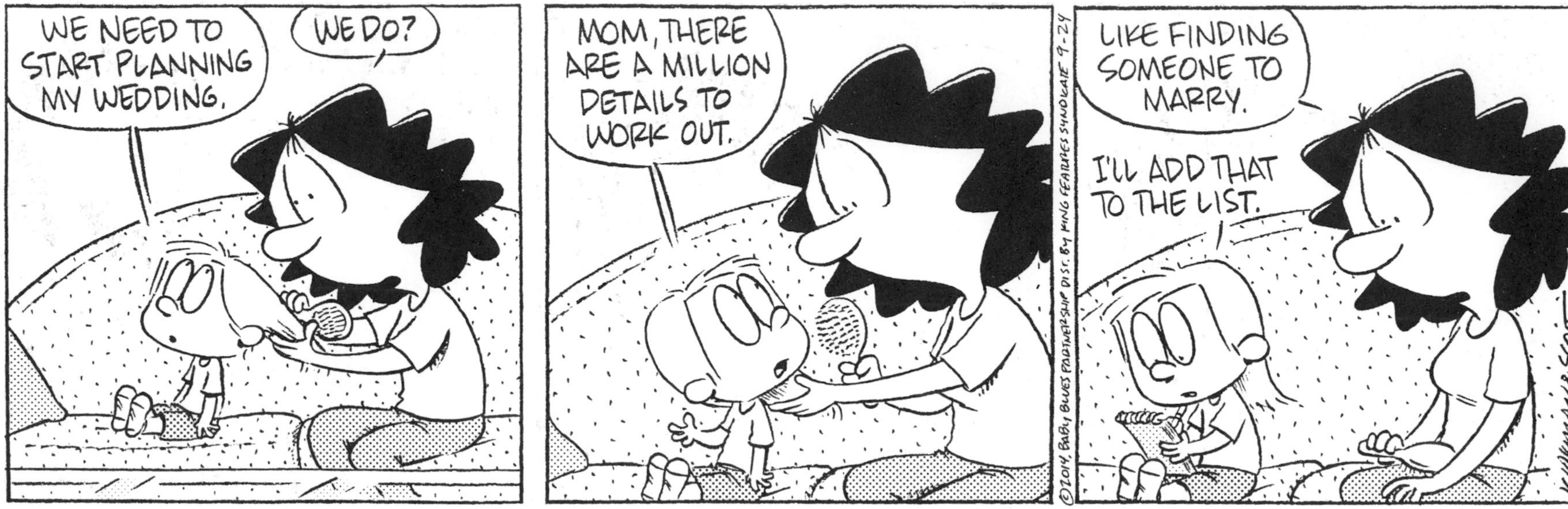
WE NEED TO START PLANNING MY WEDDING.
WE DO?
MOM, THERE ARE A MILLION DETAILS TO WORK OUT.
LIKE FINDING SOMEONE TO MARRY.
I'LL ADD THAT TO THE LIST.
©2014, BABY BLUES PARTNERSHIP DIST. BY KING FEATURES SYNDICATE 9-24
KIRKMAN & SCOTT

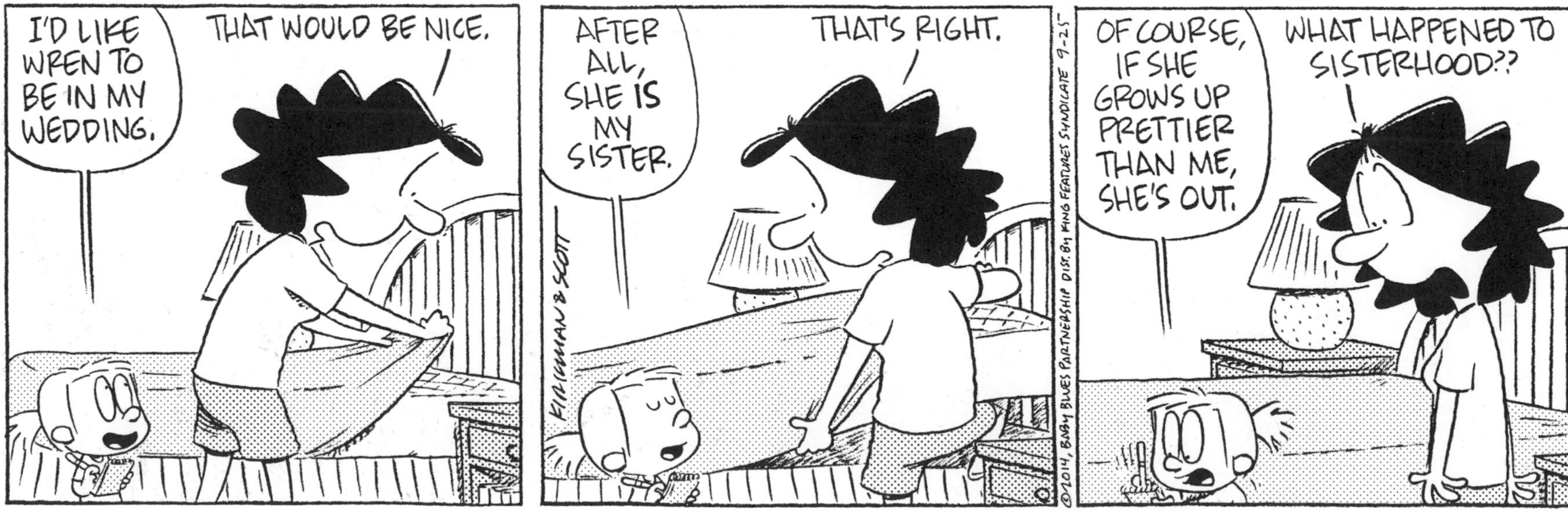
I'D LIKE WREN TO BE IN MY WEDDING.
THAT WOULD BE NICE.
AFTER ALL, SHE IS MY SISTER.
THAT'S RIGHT.
OF COURSE, IF SHE GROWS UP PRETTIER THAN ME, SHE'S OUT.
WHAT HAPPENED TO SISTERHOOD??
KIRKMAN & SCOTT
©2014, BABY BLUES PARTNERSHIP DIST. BY KING FEATURES SYNDICATE 9-25

Rick: New view of Wren's newly grown hair.

Rick: Wren's hairline grows kind of like glaciers in the Ice Age, only way faster.

Jerry: Back in the day, they used gravy. It's hard to kill the taste of something by smothering it in kale.

Rick: Amen.

Jerry: A lot happens in that second panel . . . and without words!

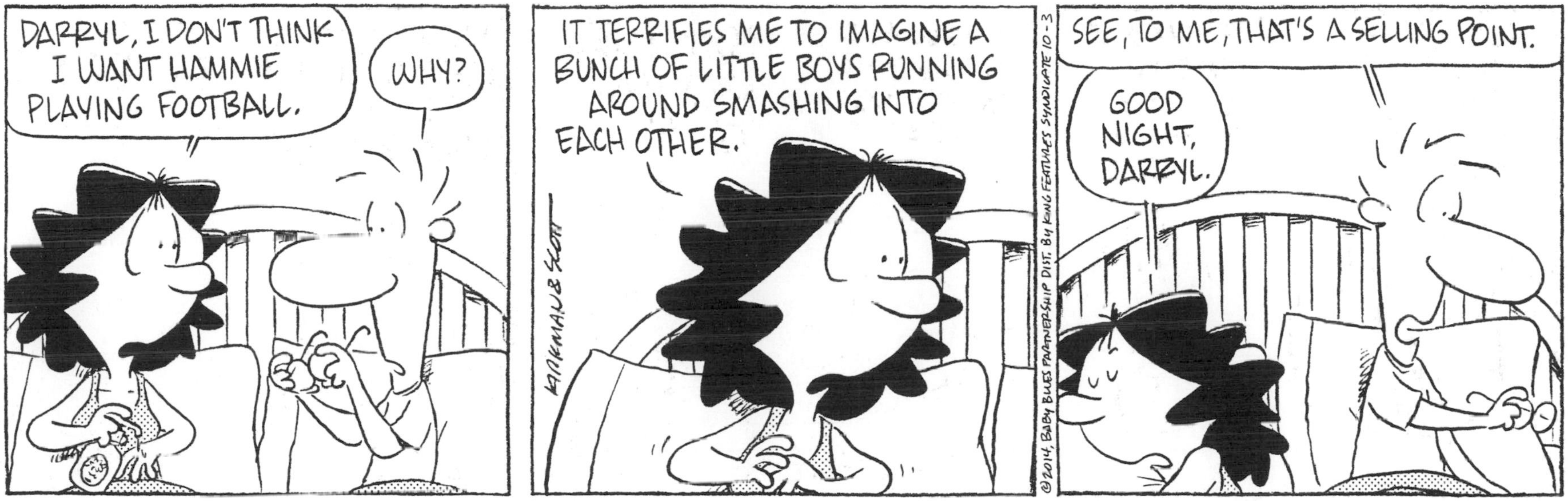
DARRYL, I DON'T THINK I WANT HAMMIE PLAYING FOOTBALL.
WHY?
IT TERRIFIES ME TO IMAGINE A BUNCH OF LITTLE BOYS RUNNING AROUND SMASHING INTO EACH OTHER.
KIRKMAN & SCOTT
©2014, BABY BLUES PARTNERSHIP DIST. BY KING FEATURES SYNDICATE 10-3
SEE, TO ME, THAT'S A SELLING POINT.
GOOD NIGHT, DARRYL.

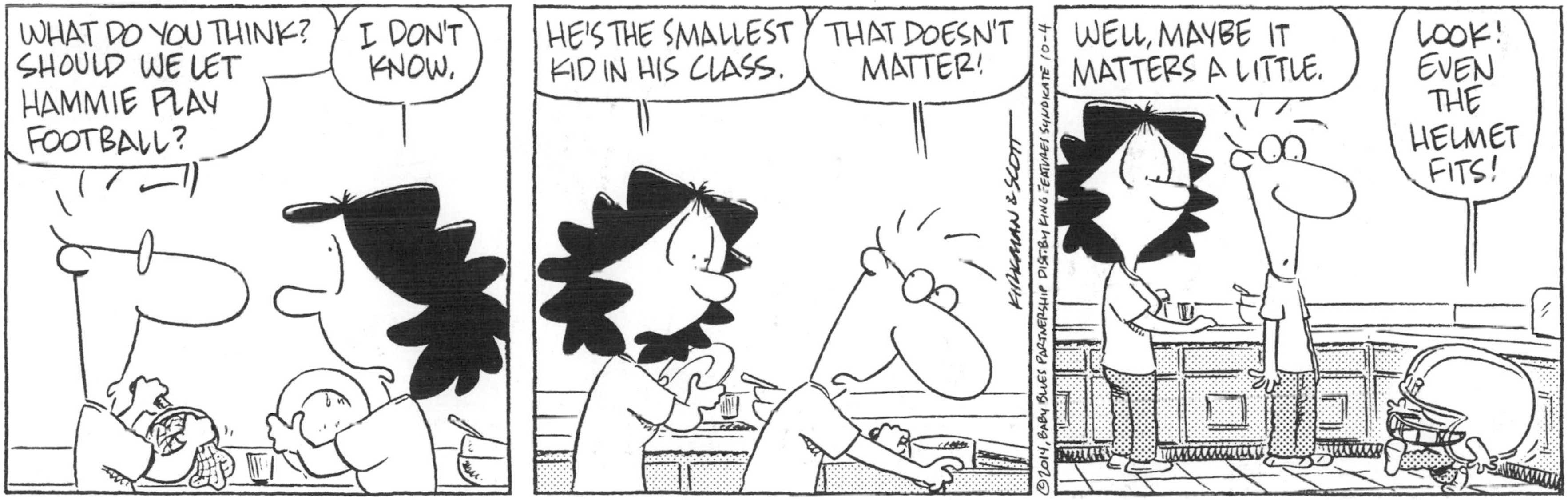
WHAT DO YOU THINK? SHOULD WE LET HAMMIE PLAY FOOTBALL?
I DON'T KNOW.
HE'S THE SMALLEST KID IN HIS CLASS.
THAT DOESN'T MATTER!
KIRKMAN & SCOTT
©2014, BABY BLUES PARTNERSHIP DIST. BY KING FEATURES SYNDICATE 10-4
WELL, MAYBE IT MATTERS A LITTLE.
LOOK! EVEN THE HELMET FITS!

Rick: I laughed out loud when I read the gag from Jerry. So funny, but so understated.

Jerry: Always listen for the fine print.

Rick: I think I shuddered when I read this description in Jerry's gag: "She is at the end of an aisle and we can see that Wren has knocked the stuff off the shelf the entire length of the aisle at her shoulder height."

Jerry: I wouldn't write strips with tons of detail in them if Rick wasn't so good at drawing them. Plus, it's kind of funny to hear him gripe about it.

Rick: This one made me chuckle before I even drew it.

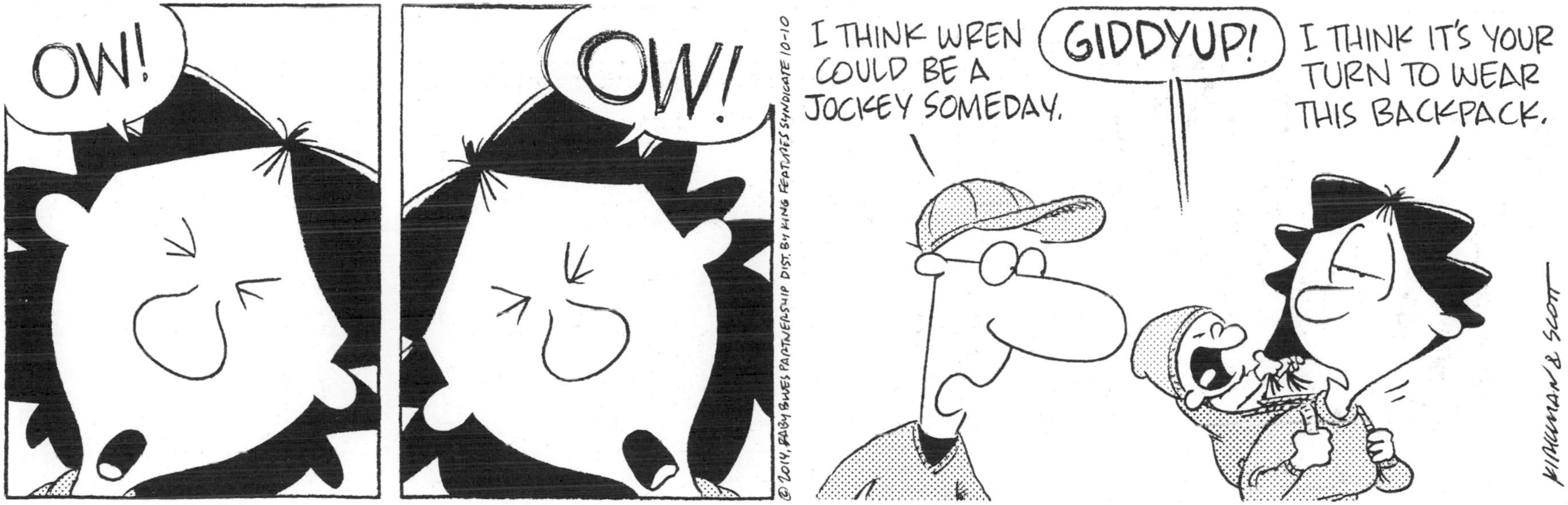
OW!
OW!
© 2014, BABY BLUES PARTNERSHIP DIST. BY KING FEATURES SYNDICATE 10-10
I THINK WREN COULD BE A JOCKEY SOMEDAY.
GIDDYUP!
I THINK IT'S YOUR TURN TO WEAR THIS BACKPACK.
KIRKMAN & SCOTT

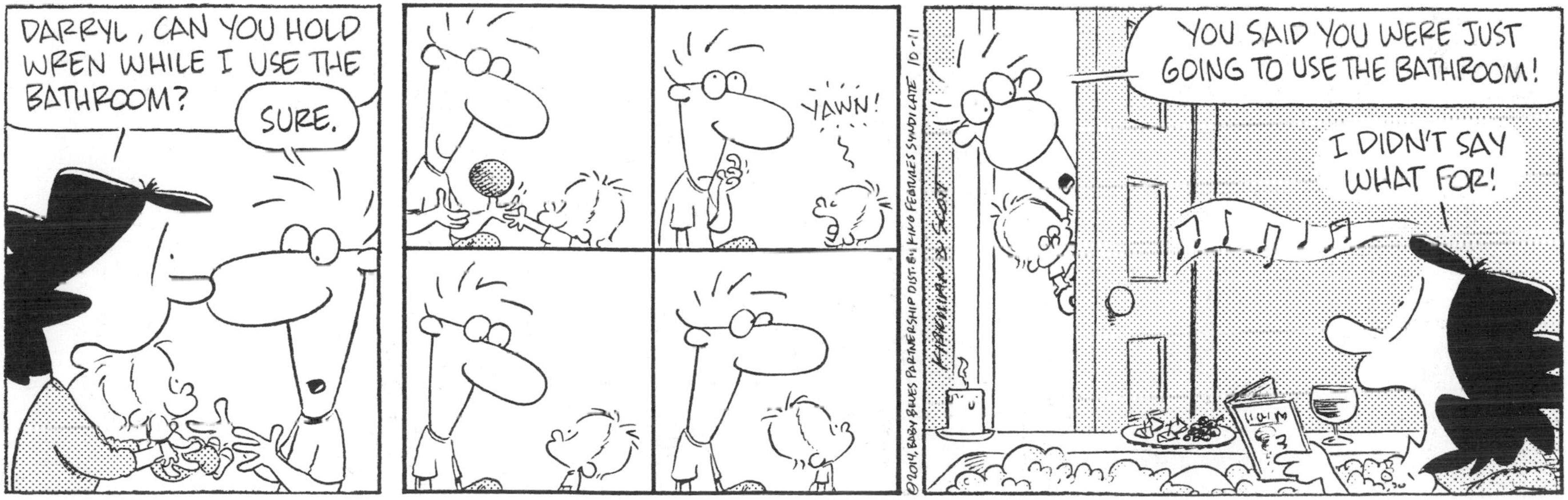
DARRYL, CAN YOU HOLD WREN WHILE I USE THE BATHROOM?
SURE.
YAWN!
© 2014, BABY BLUES PARTNERSHIP DIST. BY KING FEATURES SYNDICATE 10-11
KIRKMAN & SCOTT
YOU SAID YOU WERE JUST GOING TO USE THE BATHROOM!
I DIDN'T SAY WHAT FOR!

Rick: Title panel à la *Between Two Ferns*, with Zach Galifianakis, which is one of my favorite things on the Internet. Title panels always come last, and I had used the potted ferns to frame the panels, so naturally the web show came to mind.

Rick: But what a cool idea.

Jerry: My daughter begs me to watch a reality show with her about a veterinarian. The guy treats animals with the camera pointed directly at the most unspeakably gross parts. I mostly watch it with a pillow over my face.

Rick: "Darryl . . . navigates a maze of toys."

Jerry: The first time I was shown how to eat an artichoke, I thought I was being punked.

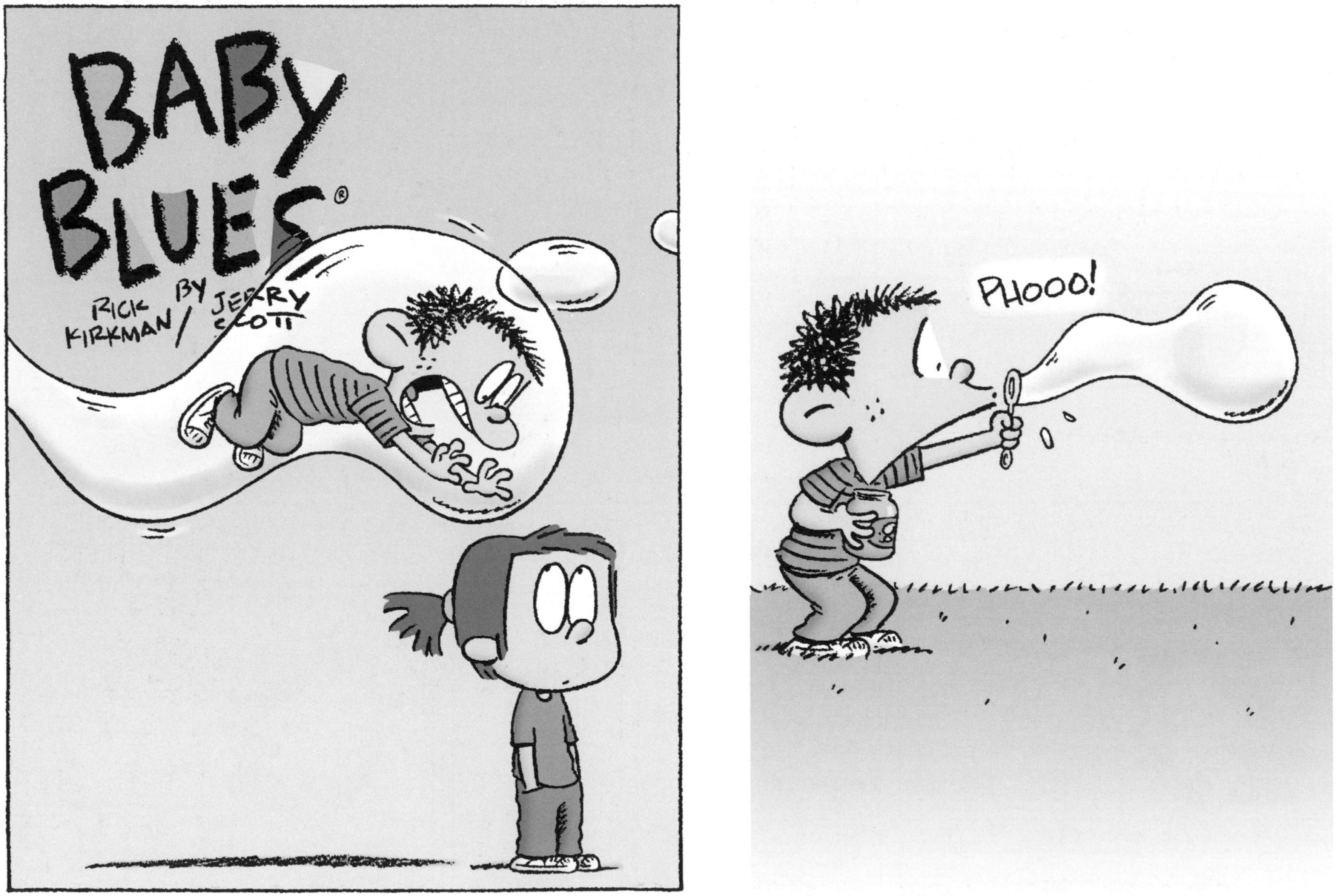
BABY BLUES®
BY RICK KIRKMAN / JERRY SCOTT
PHOOO!

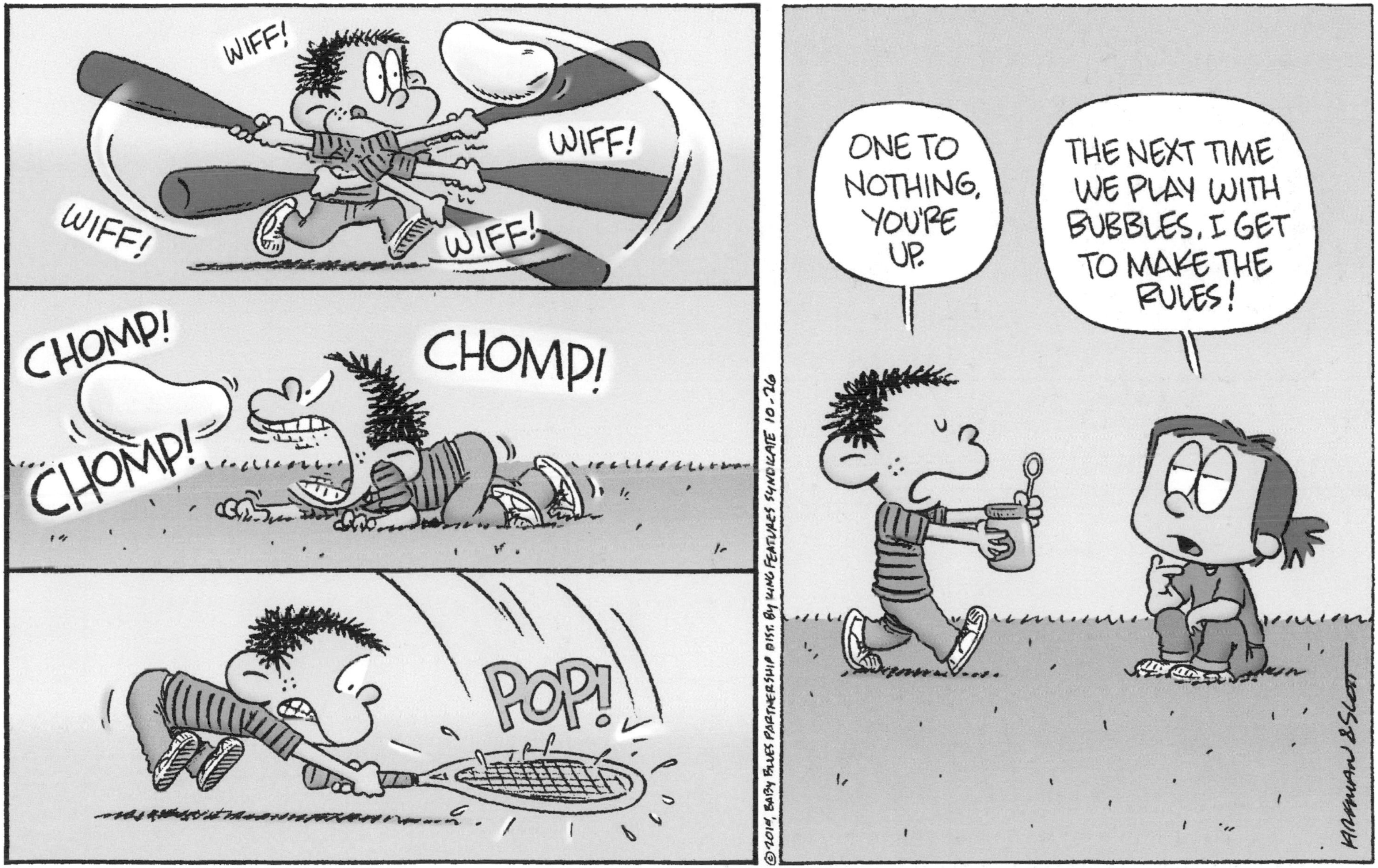
WIFF!
WIFF!
WIFF!
WIFF!
CHOMP!
CHOMP!
CHOMP!
POP!
©2014, BABY BLUES PARTNERSHIP DIST. BY KING FEATURES SYNDICATE 10-26
ONE TO NOTHING. YOU'RE UP.
THE NEXT TIME WE PLAY WITH BUBBLES, I GET TO MAKE THE RULES!
KIRKMAN & SCOTT

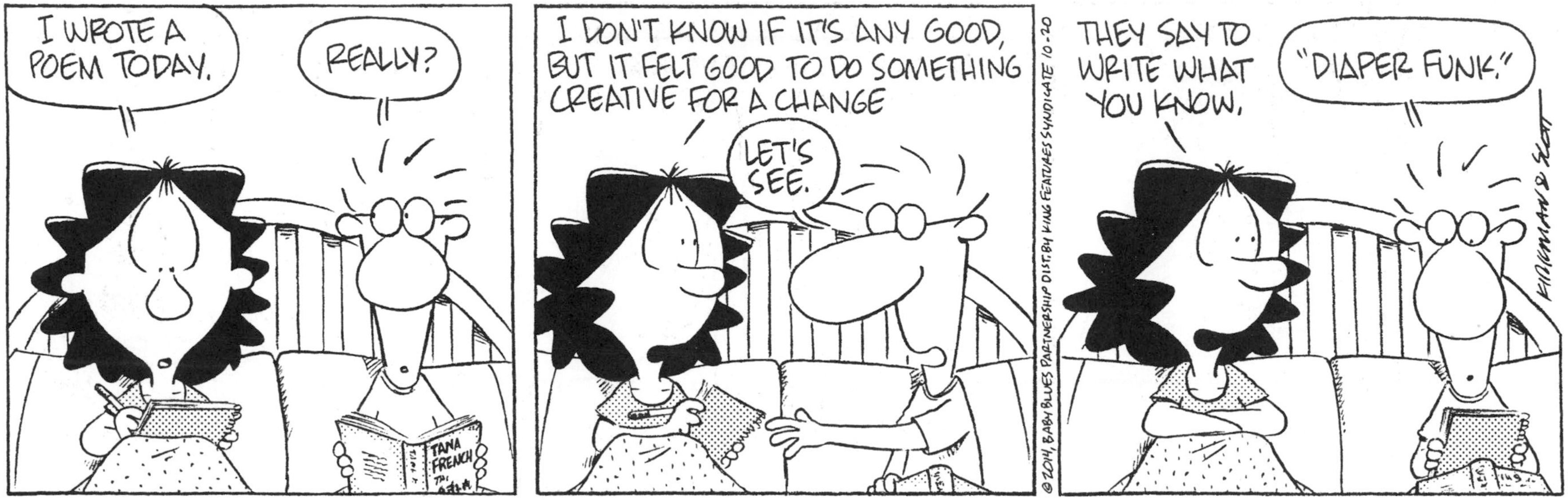
I WROTE A POEM TODAY.
REALLY?
I DON'T KNOW IF IT'S ANY GOOD, BUT IT FELT GOOD TO DO SOMETHING CREATIVE FOR A CHANGE
LET'S SEE.
THEY SAY TO WRITE WHAT YOU KNOW.
"DIAPER FUNK."
TANA FRENCH
©2014, BABY BLUES PARTNERSHIP DIST. BY KING FEATURES SYNDICATE 10-20
KIRKMAN & SCOTT

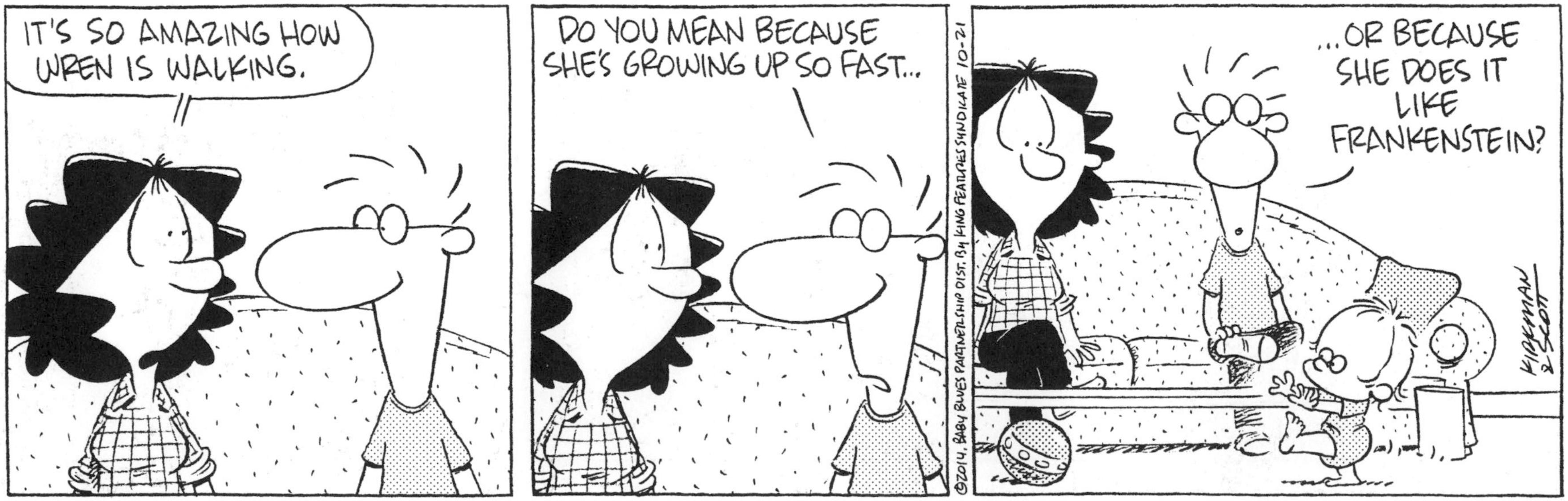
IT'S SO AMAZING HOW WREN IS WALKING.
DO YOU MEAN BECAUSE SHE'S GROWING UP SO FAST...
...OR BECAUSE SHE DOES IT LIKE FRANKENSTEIN?
©2014, BABY BLUES PARTNERSHIP DIST. BY KING FEATURES SYNDICATE 10-21
KIRKMAN & SCOTT

Jerry: The editors must have been absent the day that one ran.

Jerry: Been there, felt like that.

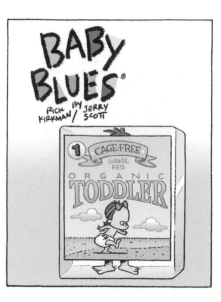

Rick: For the guy on the bench, I started by basing it on Jerry's dad and tweaking it from there.

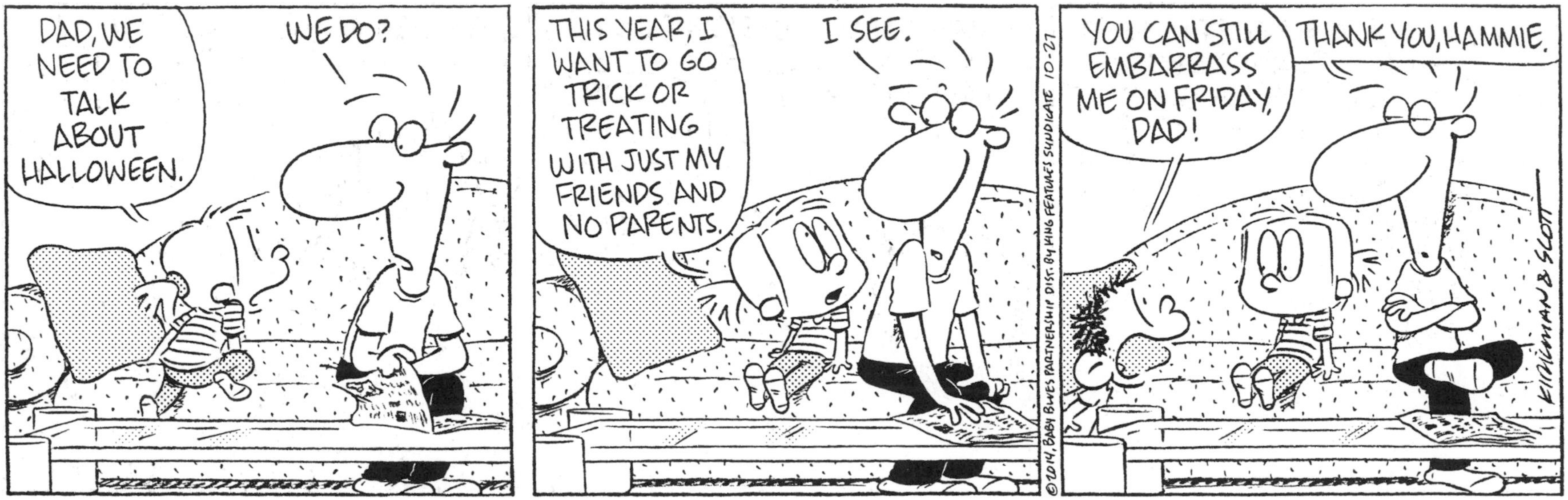
DAD, WE NEED TO TALK ABOUT HALLOWEEN.
WE DO?
THIS YEAR, I WANT TO GO TRICK OR TREATING WITH JUST MY FRIENDS AND NO PARENTS.
I SEE.
©2014, BABY BLUES PARTNERSHIP DIST. BY KING FEATURES SYNDICATE 10-27
YOU CAN STILL EMBARRASS ME ON FRIDAY, DAD!
THANK YOU, HAMMIE.
KIRKMAN & SCOTT

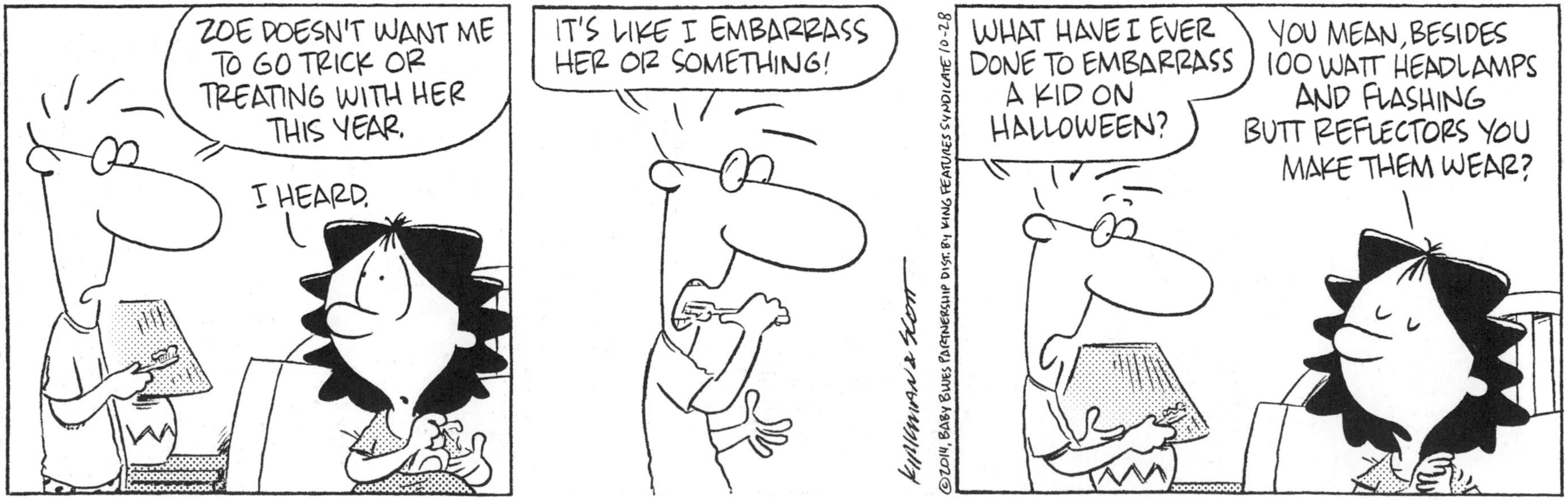
ZOE DOESN'T WANT ME TO GO TRICK OR TREATING WITH HER THIS YEAR.
I HEARD.
IT'S LIKE I EMBARRASS HER OR SOMETHING!
KIRKMAN & SCOTT
©2014, BABY BLUES PARTNERSHIP DIST. BY KING FEATURES SYNDICATE 10-28
WHAT HAVE I EVER DONE TO EMBARRASS A KID ON HALLOWEEN?
YOU MEAN, BESIDES 100 WATT HEADLAMPS AND FLASHING BUTT REFLECTORS YOU MAKE THEM WEAR?

Rick: Darryl could learn a lot from lawyers. They know not to ask a question if they don't already know the answer. Darryl's Corollary: Never agree to a costume if you don't know what it is first.

Jerry: Right. The key is the detail.

Jerry: Darryl MacPherson: Really good dad, butt-ugly BRONY.

Jerry: Wanda was obviously a child in a time before weather apps.

Rick: I think this must be the oddest panel I've ever drawn. You think it looks weird here . . . the black-and-white line art makes even less sense.

Jerry: I love the first panel in this strip. It doesn't really make any sense until you read the second panel, then go back and look at it again.

171

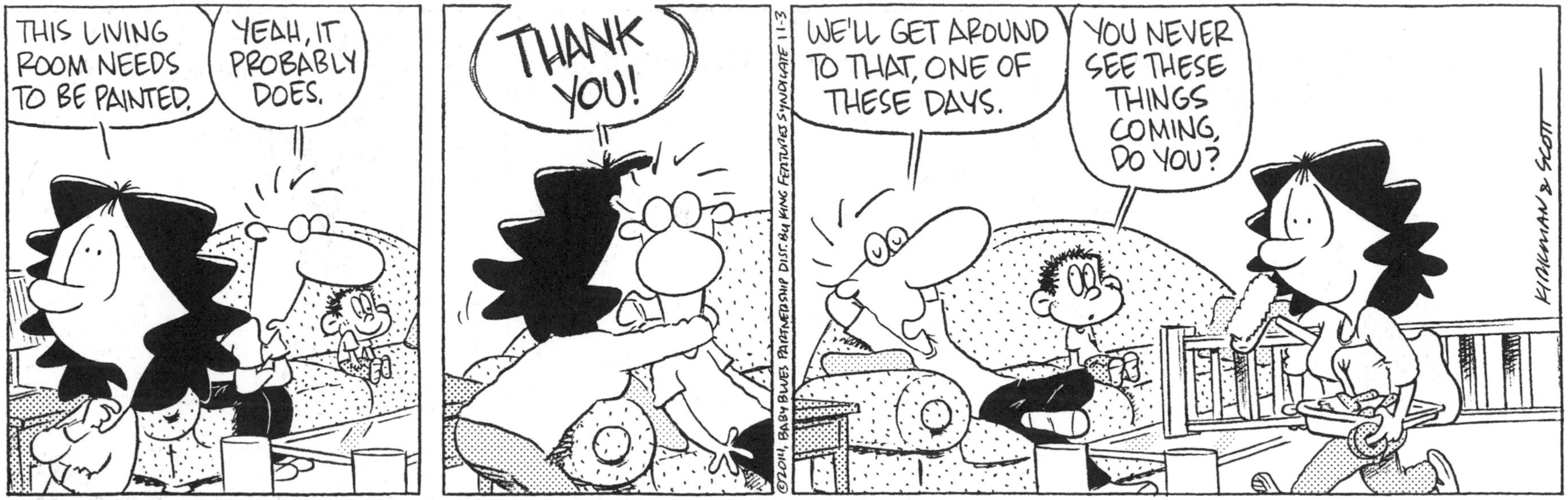

THIS LIVING ROOM NEEDS TO BE PAINTED.
YEAH, IT PROBABLY DOES.
THANK YOU!
©2014, BABY BLUES PARTNERSHIP DIST. BY KING FEATURES SYNDICATE 11-3
WE'LL GET AROUND TO THAT, ONE OF THESE DAYS.
YOU NEVER SEE THESE THINGS COMING, DO YOU?
KIRKMAN & SCOTT

Jerry: We were in the middle of a home improvement project when the idea for this series came to me. Our project started with the idea of moving the TV to a different wall. By the time it was over, we had replaced all of the furniture, window coverings, repainted the entire house, and remodeled the kitchen. Sheesh.

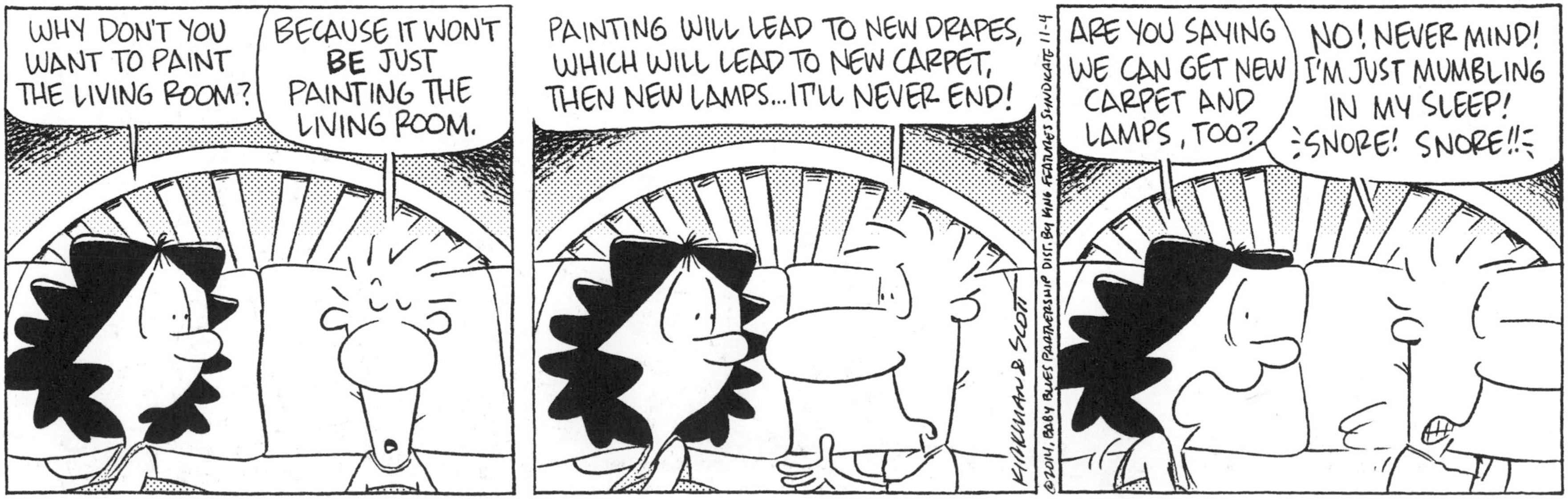

WHY DON'T YOU WANT TO PAINT THE LIVING ROOM?
BECAUSE IT WON'T **BE** JUST PAINTING THE LIVING ROOM.
PAINTING WILL LEAD TO NEW DRAPES, WHICH WILL LEAD TO NEW CARPET, THEN NEW LAMPS... IT'LL NEVER END!
KIRKMAN & SCOTT
©2014, BABY BLUES PARTNERSHIP DIST. BY KING FEATURES SYNDICATE 11-4
ARE YOU SAYING WE CAN GET NEW CARPET AND LAMPS, TOO?
NO! NEVER MIND! I'M JUST MUMBLING IN MY SLEEP! SNORE! SNORE!!

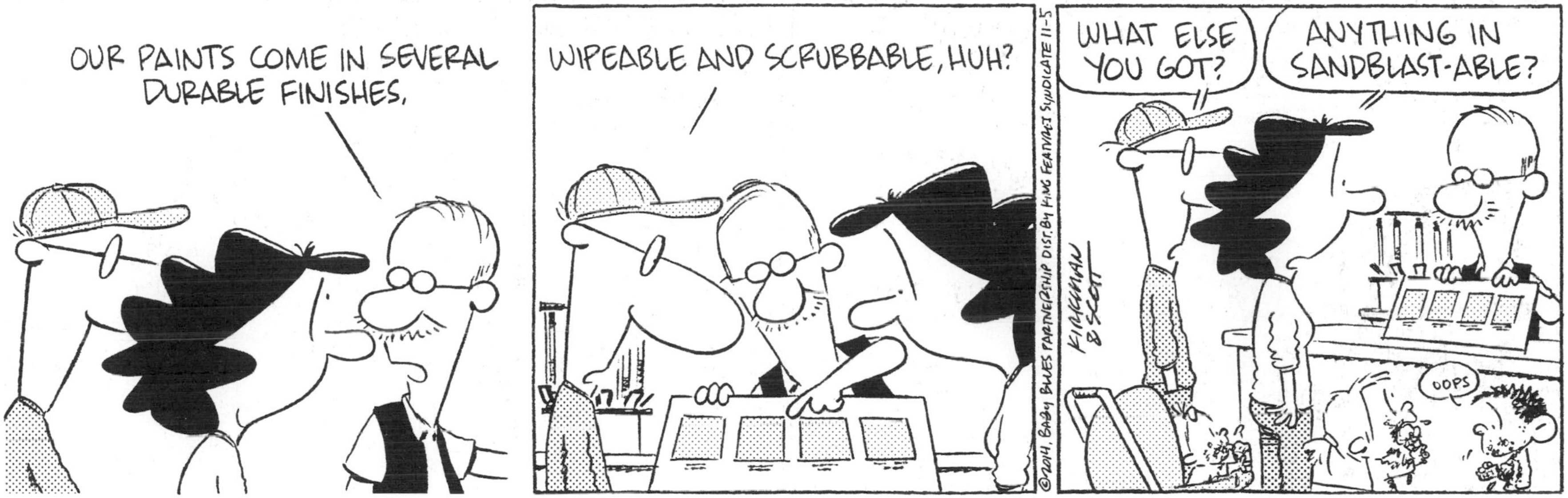
OUR PAINTS COME IN SEVERAL DURABLE FINISHES.
WIPEABLE AND SCRUBBABLE, HUH?
©2014, BABY BLUES PARTNERSHIP DIST. BY KING FEATURES SYNDICATE 11-5
KIRKMAN & SCOTT
WHAT ELSE YOU GOT?
ANYTHING IN SANDBLAST-ABLE?
OOPS

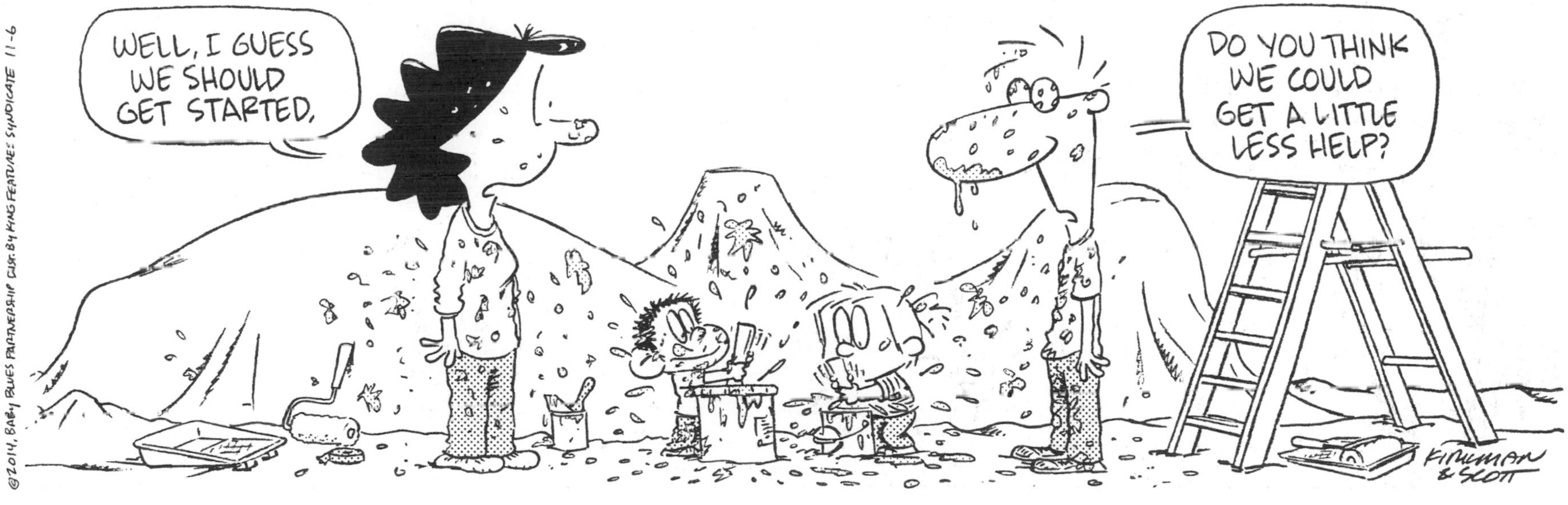
©2014, BABY BLUES PARTNERSHIP DIST. BY KING FEATURES SYNDICATE 11-6
WELL, I GUESS WE SHOULD GET STARTED.
DO YOU THINK WE COULD GET A LITTLE LESS HELP?
KIRKMAN & SCOTT

Rick: This series is an example of one of Jerry's great skills. He can do a series of gags, which can all stand alone and have a joke in them every day, but still have told a contained story by the end of the series. Way easier said than done.

Rick: Darryl barks call signals based on a compilation video of bizarre Peyton Manning calls.

Rick: I love it when Hammie is so clueless . . .

Jerry: Nobody makes the I-Have-an-Annoying-Little-Brother face like Zoe.

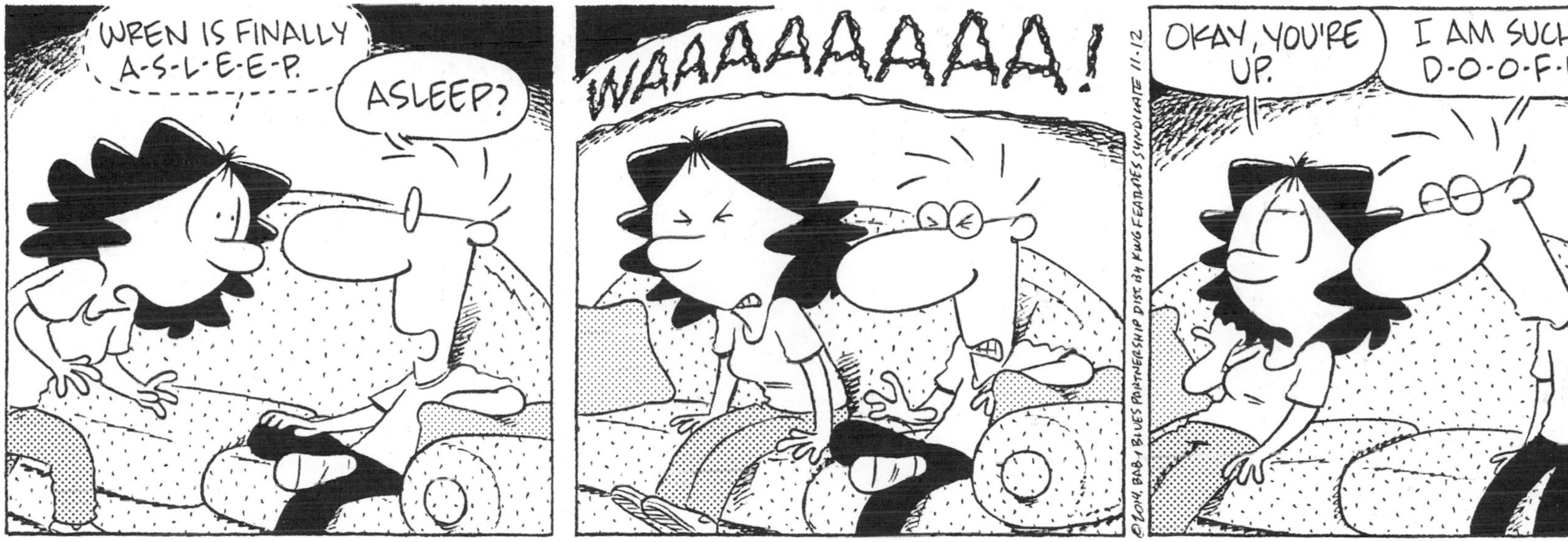
WREN IS FINALLY A-S-L-E-E-P.
ASLEEP?
WAAAAAAAAA!
© 2014 BABY BLUES PARTNERSHIP DIST. BY KING FEATURES SYNDICATE 11-12
OKAY, YOU'RE UP.
I AM SUCH A D-O-O-F-U-S.
KIRKMAN & SCOTT

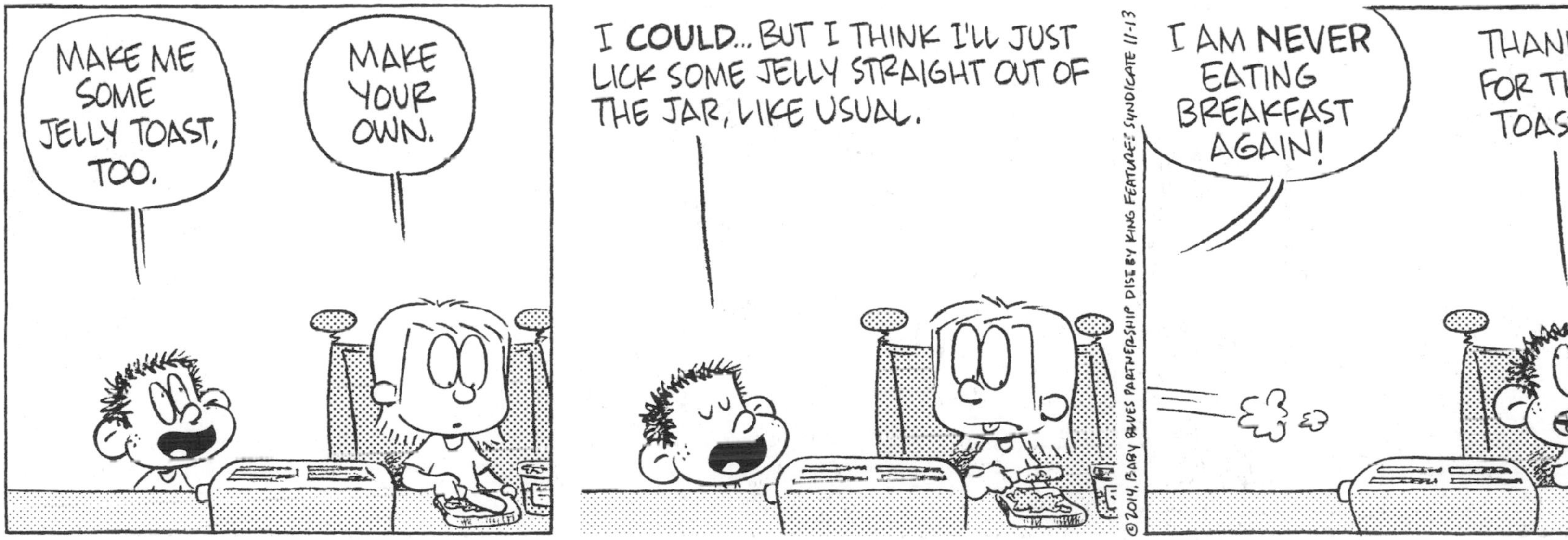
MAKE ME SOME JELLY TOAST, TOO.
MAKE YOUR OWN.
I **COULD**... BUT I THINK I'LL JUST LICK SOME JELLY STRAIGHT OUT OF THE JAR, LIKE USUAL.
© 2014, BABY BLUES PARTNERSHIP DIST. BY KING FEATURES SYNDICATE 11-13
I AM **NEVER** EATING BREAKFAST AGAIN!
THANKS FOR THE TOAST.
KIRKMAN & SCOTT

Rick:. . . and yet so savvy.

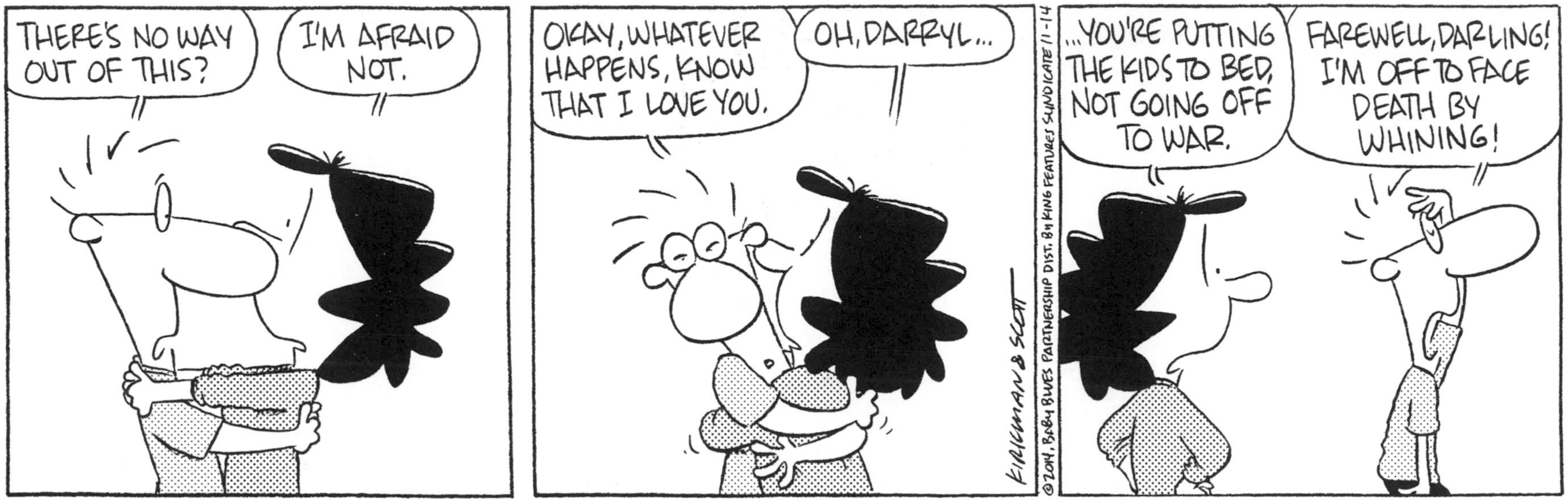
THERE'S NO WAY OUT OF THIS?
I'M AFRAID NOT.
OKAY, WHATEVER HAPPENS, KNOW THAT I LOVE YOU.
OH, DARRYL...
KIRKMAN & SCOTT
©2014, BABY BLUES PARTNERSHIP DIST. BY KING FEATURES SYNDICATE 11-14
...YOU'RE PUTTING THE KIDS TO BED, NOT GOING OFF TO WAR.
FAREWELL, DARLING! I'M OFF TO FACE DEATH BY WHINING!

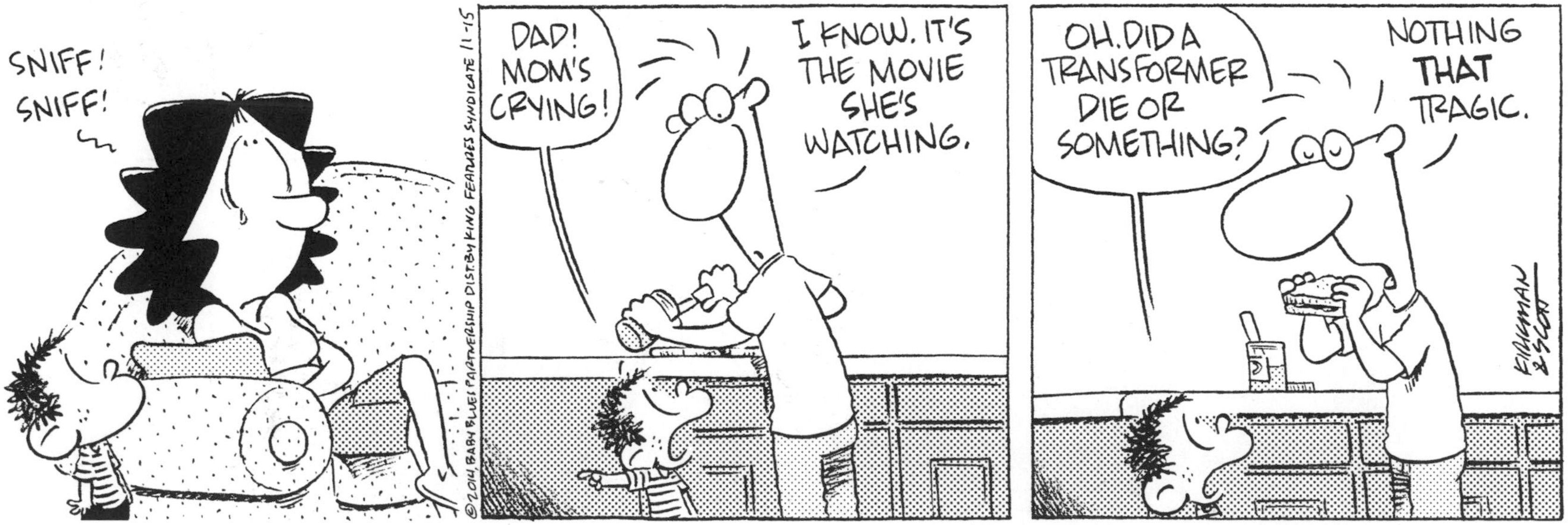
SNIFF! SNIFF!
©2014 BABY BLUES PARTNERSHIP DIST. BY KING FEATURES SYNDICATE 11-15
DAD! MOM'S CRYING!
I KNOW. IT'S THE MOVIE SHE'S WATCHING.
OH. DID A TRANSFORMER DIE OR SOMETHING?
NOTHING **THAT** TRAGIC.
KIRKMAN & SCOTT

Rick: You get used to a lot of things when you have kids.

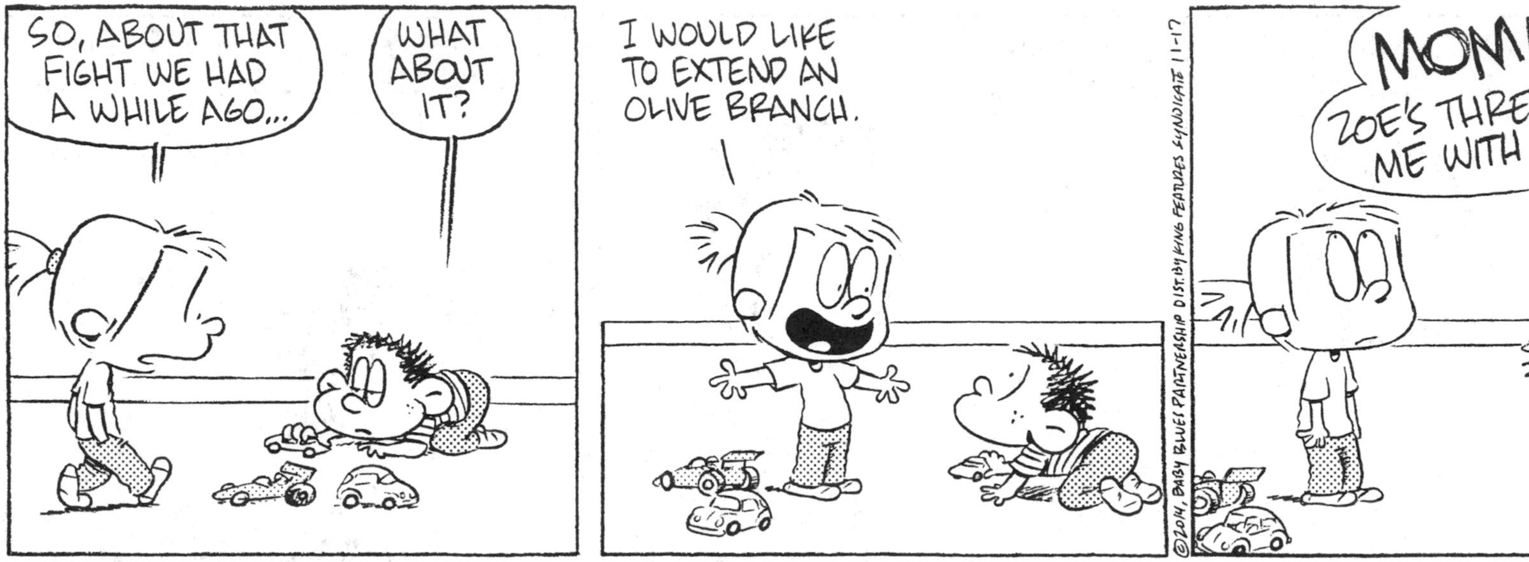
SO, ABOUT THAT FIGHT WE HAD A WHILE AGO...
WHAT ABOUT IT?
I WOULD LIKE TO EXTEND AN OLIVE BRANCH.
© 2014, BABY BLUES PARTNERSHIP DIST. BY KING FEATURES SYNDICATE 11-17
MOM!!
ZOE'S THREATENING ME WITH A STICK!
KIRKMAN & SCOTT

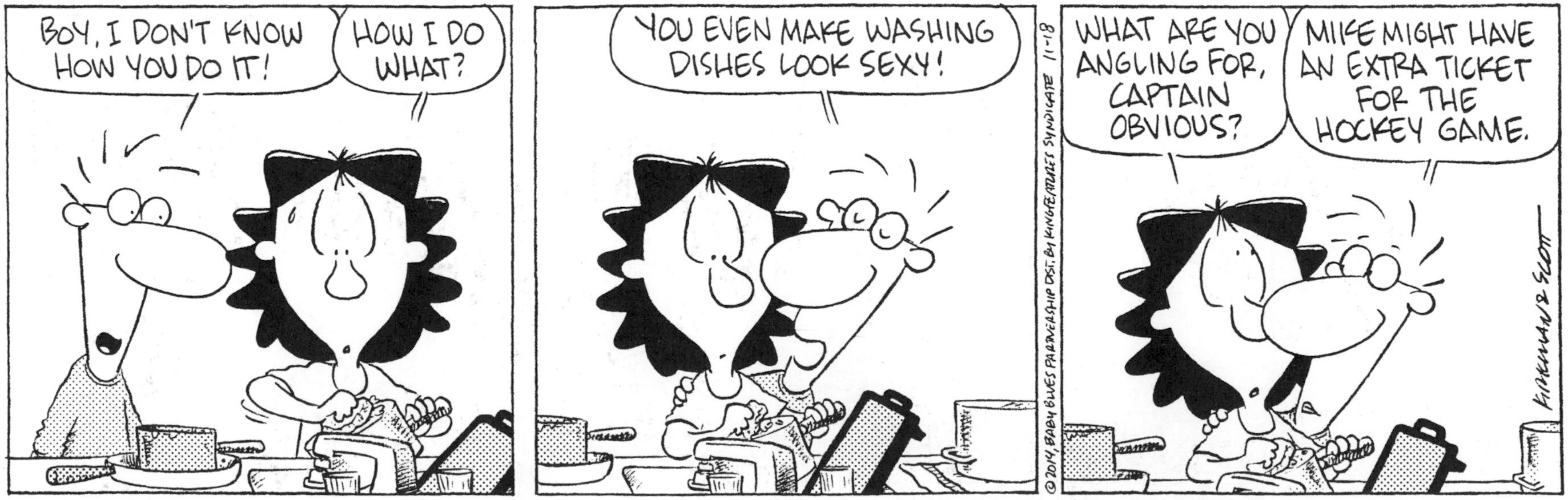
BOY, I DON'T KNOW HOW YOU DO IT!
HOW I DO WHAT?
YOU EVEN MAKE WASHING DISHES LOOK SEXY!
© 2014, BABY BLUES PARTNERSHIP DIST. BY KING FEATURES SYNDICATE 11-18
WHAT ARE YOU ANGLING FOR, CAPTAIN OBVIOUS?
MIKE MIGHT HAVE AN EXTRA TICKET FOR THE HOCKEY GAME.
KIRKMAN & SCOTT

Jerry: Sometimes you have to work with what you've got.

Rick: As long as you go through Hazmat decontamination afterward.

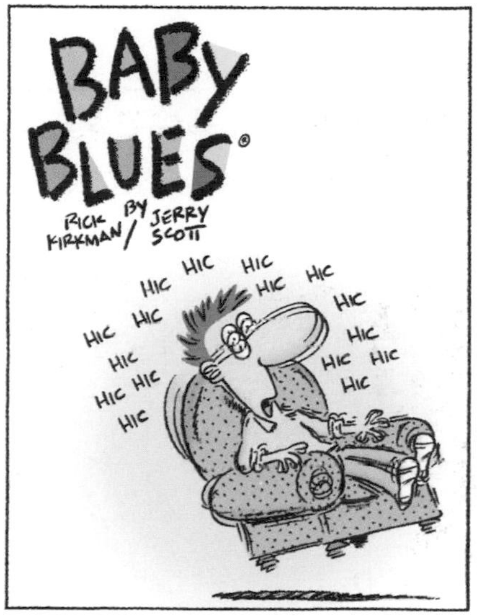
BABY BLUES®
RICK KIRKMAN / BY JERRY SCOTT
HIC HIC HIC HIC HIC
HIC HIC HIC HIC
HIC HIC HIC HIC
HIC HIC HIC HIC

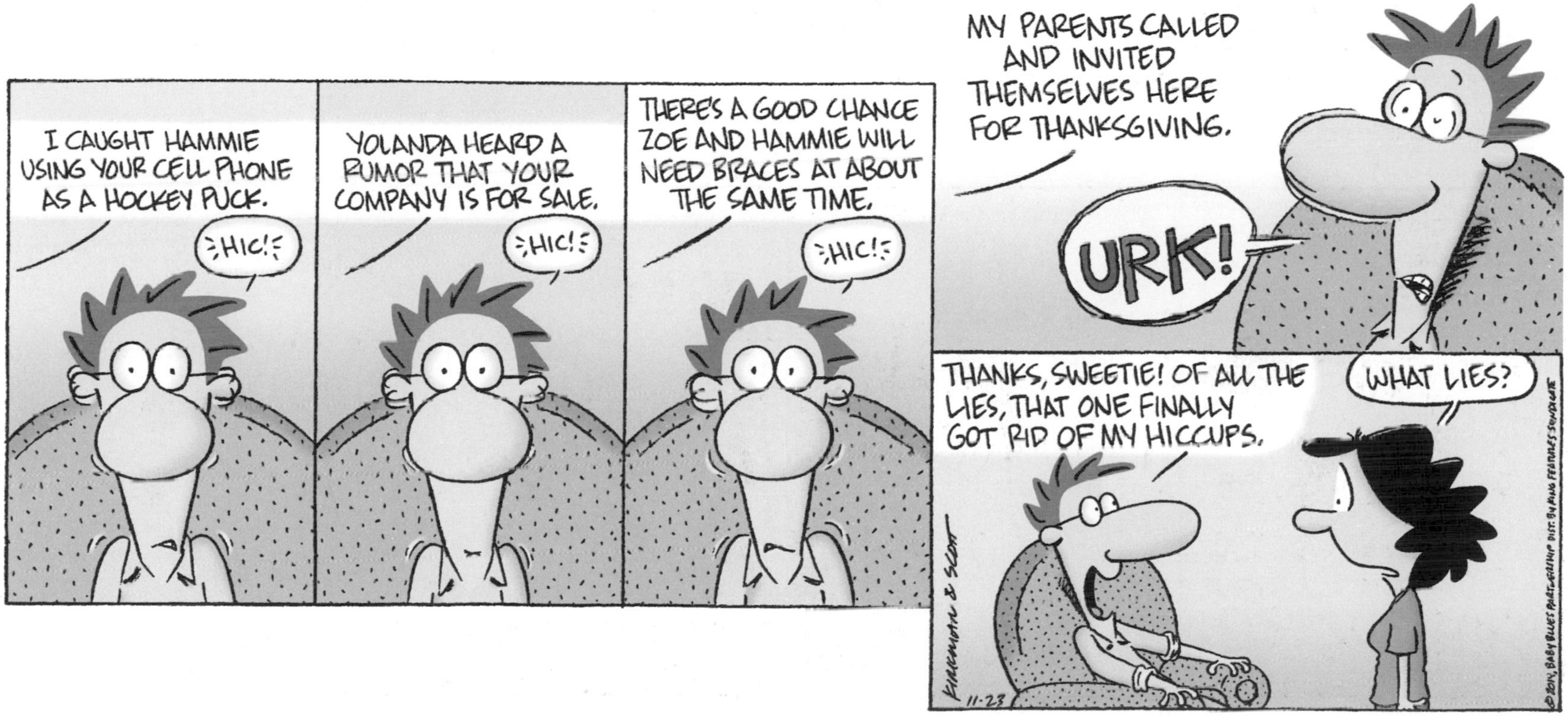
I CAUGHT HAMMIE USING YOUR CELL PHONE AS A HOCKEY PUCK.
HIC!
YOLANDA HEARD A RUMOR THAT YOUR COMPANY IS FOR SALE.
HIC!
THERE'S A GOOD CHANCE ZOE AND HAMMIE WILL NEED BRACES AT ABOUT THE SAME TIME.
HIC!
MY PARENTS CALLED AND INVITED THEMSELVES HERE FOR THANKSGIVING.
URK!
THANKS, SWEETIE! OF ALL THE LIES, THAT ONE FINALLY GOT RID OF MY HICCUPS.
WHAT LIES?
KIRKMAN & SCOTT
11-23

Jerry: Right. And what was with the big buckles on the hats and shoes?

Jerry: We considered having a Darryl parade balloon made, but the nose wouldn't fit between the buildings on Sixth Avenue.

SNOT.

Rick: We did get one tirade—I mean, comment—from a reader that started off: "What in God's name were you thinking when you drew the Thanksgiving Day strip?" It just went downhill from there.

Jerry: I think we should see more of the grandparents in the strip. If you agree, send us an email from the babyblues.com web site.

Jerry: We had an early Christmas once when we pulled the kids' beds out and found all the stuff that had been stuck between the mattress and tho wall.

Rick: Always an agenda lurking.

Rick: Part of me hopes he'll never learn.

Rick: Scared me just to draw it.

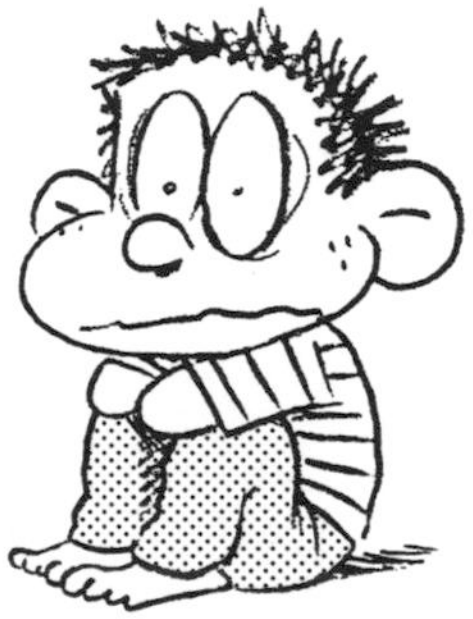

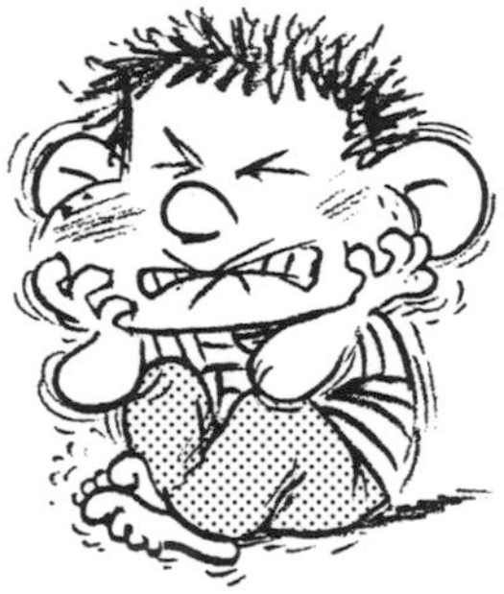

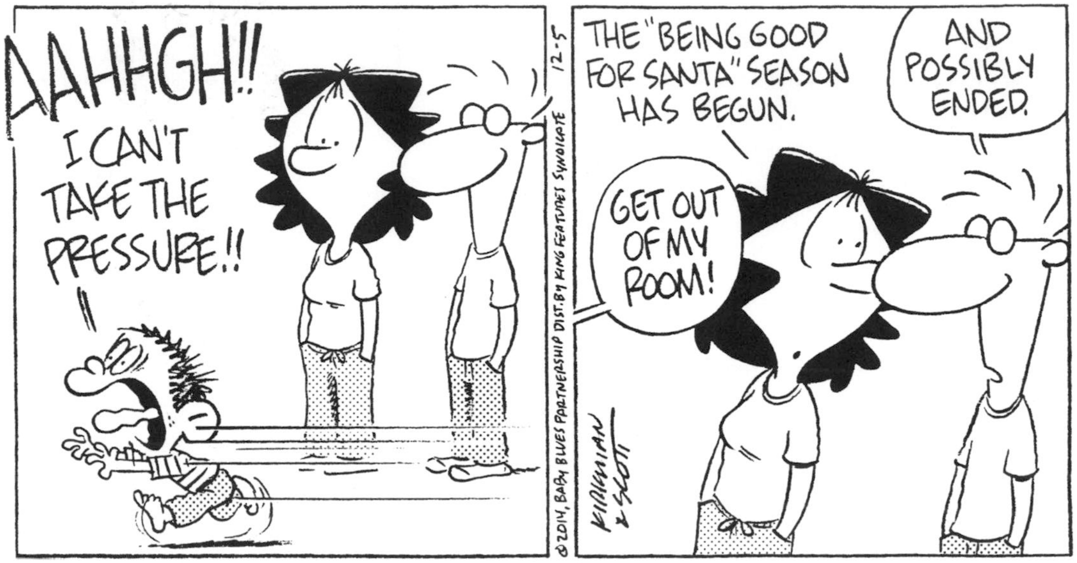
AAHHGH!! I CAN'T TAKE THE PRESSURE!!
12-5
©2014, BABY BLUES PARTNERSHIP DIST. BY KING FEATURES SYNDICATE
KIRKMAN & SCOTT
THE "BEING GOOD FOR SANTA" SEASON HAS BEGUN.
GET OUT OF MY ROOM!
AND POSSIBLY ENDED.

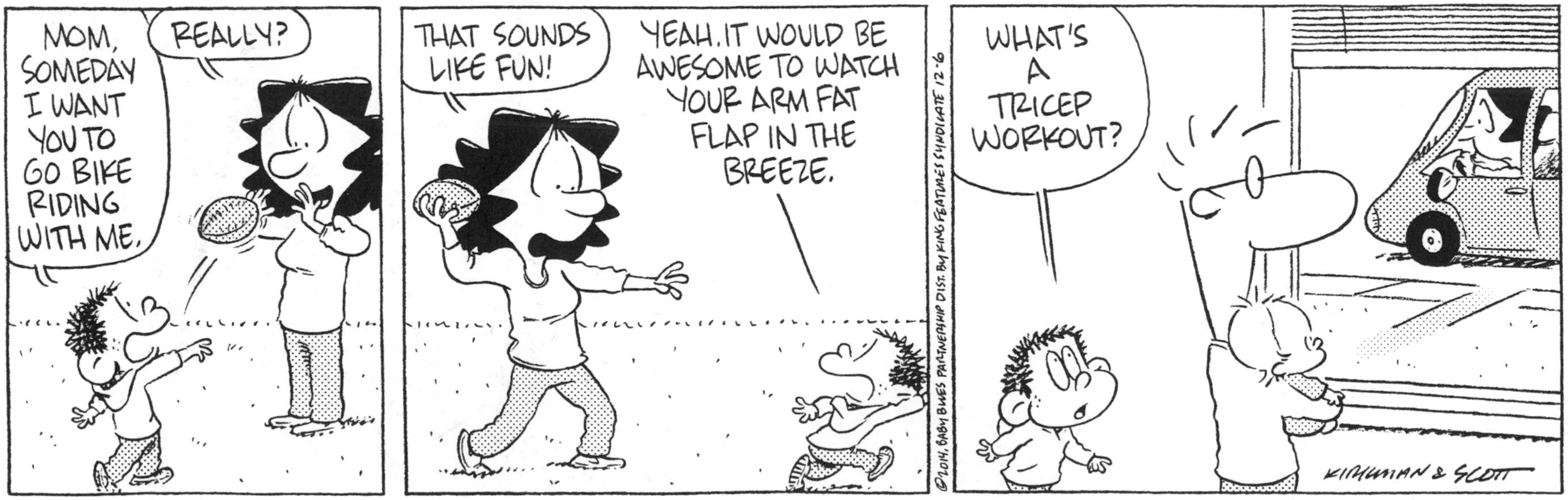
MOM, SOMEDAY I WANT YOU TO GO BIKE RIDING WITH ME.
REALLY?
THAT SOUNDS LIKE FUN!
YEAH. IT WOULD BE AWESOME TO WATCH YOUR ARM FAT FLAP IN THE BREEZE.
©2014, BABY BLUES PARTNERSHIP DIST. BY KING FEATURES SYNDICATE 12-6
WHAT'S A TRICEP WORKOUT?
KIRKMAN & SCOTT

Rick: I do like it when we leave it to the reader to connect the dots to get the gag.

Rick: I trotted out an old co-worker, Stan, who was based on a real friend of ours. I had seen him recently and decided to update him in the strip, although the real Stan now has a beard.

Rick: We were severely chastised by readers over these two strips—and rightly so, if we're to be considered example-setters.

Rick: Kids in car seats should not be in the front seat. But everyone has their lapses and gives in to pressure from their kids. Luckily, this time was uneventful, and it won't happen again.

Jerry: We're finding new opportunities for action in the strip as Wren gets more and more mobile. We may have to rent some space from another comic strip to fit it all in.

Rick: Writing samples: My older daughter's list of ideas from her and her sister—I have no idea what that was all about—and my younger daughter's Mother's Day card. When you care enough to steal from the very best.

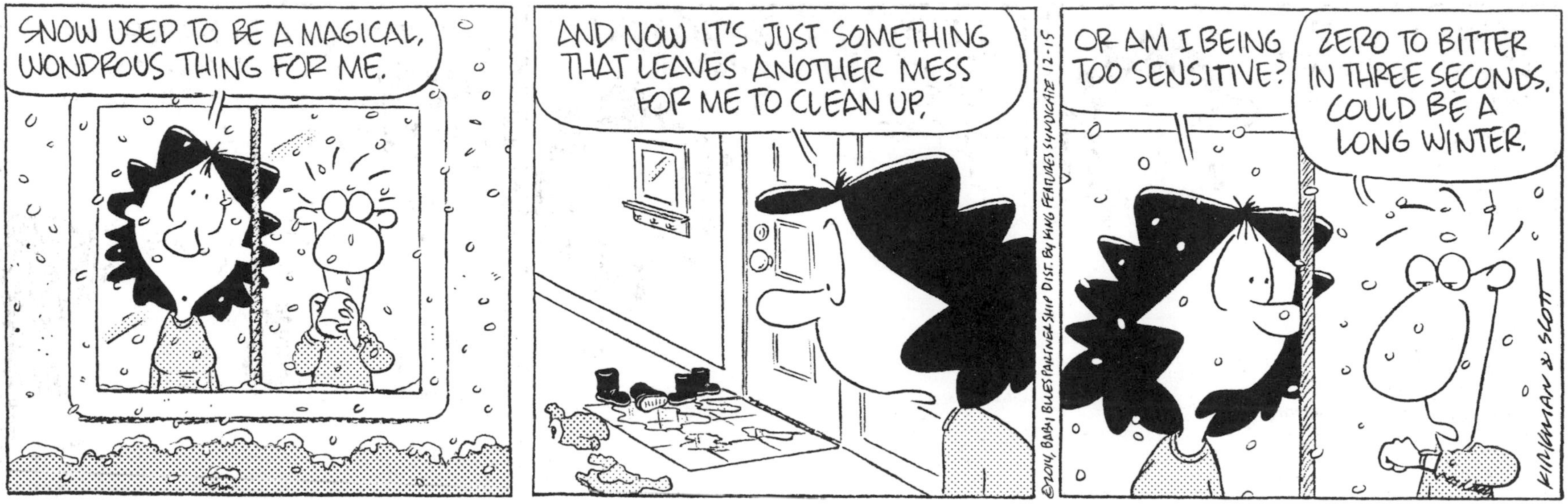
SNOW USED TO BE A MAGICAL, WONDROUS THING FOR ME.
AND NOW IT'S JUST SOMETHING THAT LEAVES ANOTHER MESS FOR ME TO CLEAN UP.
©2014, BABY BLUES PARTNERSHIP DIST. BY KING FEATURES SYNDICATE 12-15
OR AM I BEING TOO SENSITIVE?
ZERO TO BITTER IN THREE SECONDS. COULD BE A LONG WINTER.
KIRKMAN & SCOTT

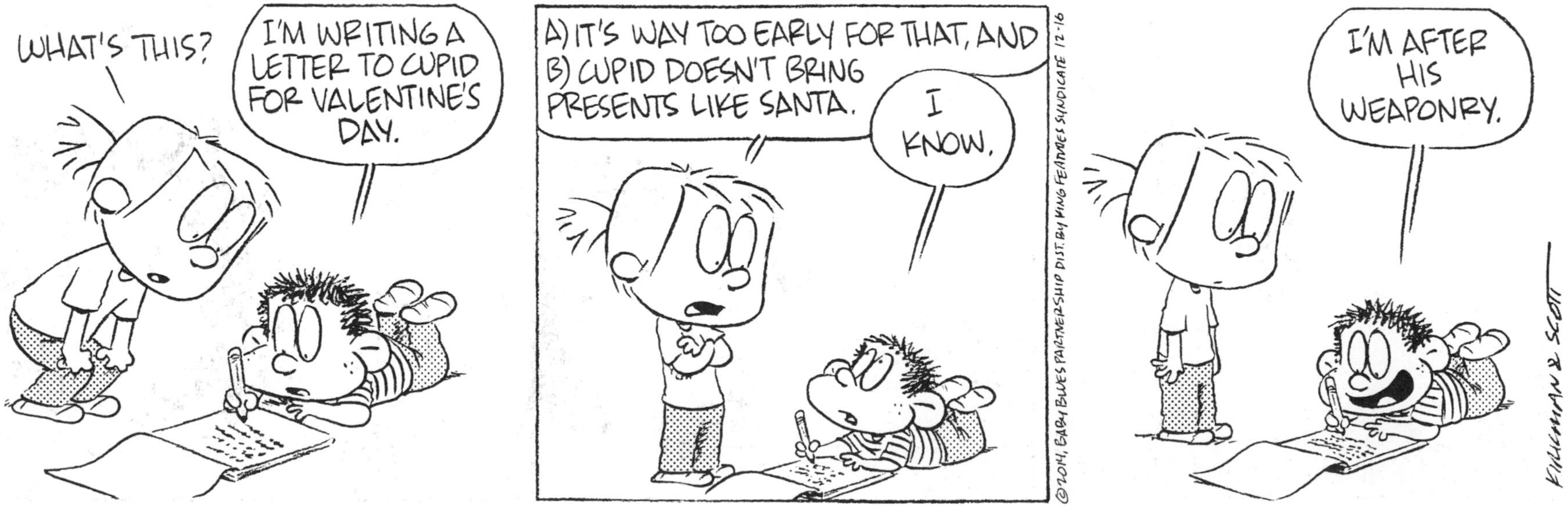
WHAT'S THIS?
I'M WRITING A LETTER TO CUPID FOR VALENTINE'S DAY.
A) IT'S WAY TOO EARLY FOR THAT, AND B) CUPID DOESN'T BRING PRESENTS LIKE SANTA.
I KNOW.
©2014, BABY BLUES PARTNERSHIP DIST. BY KING FEATURES SYNDICATE 12-16
I'M AFTER HIS WEAPONRY.
KIRKMAN & SCOTT

Panel 1:
GOOD! I THINK YOU'VE GOT IT, WREN!
GOT WHAT?

Panel 2:
I JUST TAUGHT WREN HER FIRST FULL SENTENCE.
REALLY? MAY I HEAR IT?

Panel 3:
HAMMIE DIDDIT!
I THOUGHT I SHOULD START WITH THE BASICS.

Panel 4:
WHAT'S FOR DINNER?
THAT CHICKEN STUFF I ALWAYS MAKE.

Panel 5:
OH. CAN I HAVE SOME CANDY?
IT'LL SPOIL YOUR DINNER.

Panel 6:
SO WE'RE ON THE SAME PAGE.

Jerry: One of the great privileges of fatherhood is the right to totally make up facts to support your arguments.

Rick: Well, I love any time when we include a reference to The Beatles. Combining two of the most famous noses in the title panel was a natural. Sorry, Ringo. And I love the new reindeer names. I'm hoping it starts a tradition.

Jerry: It's cool how drawing the same characters two or three times in a single panel reads as movement and chaos.

Jerry: Flying reindeer, breaking and entering, unattended packages . . . I have a lot of questions about the story, too, Zoe.

Rick: At some point I think we just gave up on trying to capture it.

Jerry: Everybody should be outstanding at something.

Rick: I found laser tag birthdays to be utterly exhausting. And smelly. A lot of fun to draw Hammie's action sequence, though.

Jerry: One game of laser tag with a bunch of seventh graders was all it took to convince me that I'll never star in an action movie.

Jerry: Somehow, sometime, your kid's reading list will jump from *Clifford the Big Red Dog* to *Charlotte's Web* to gender-bending vampire romance novels. Be ready.

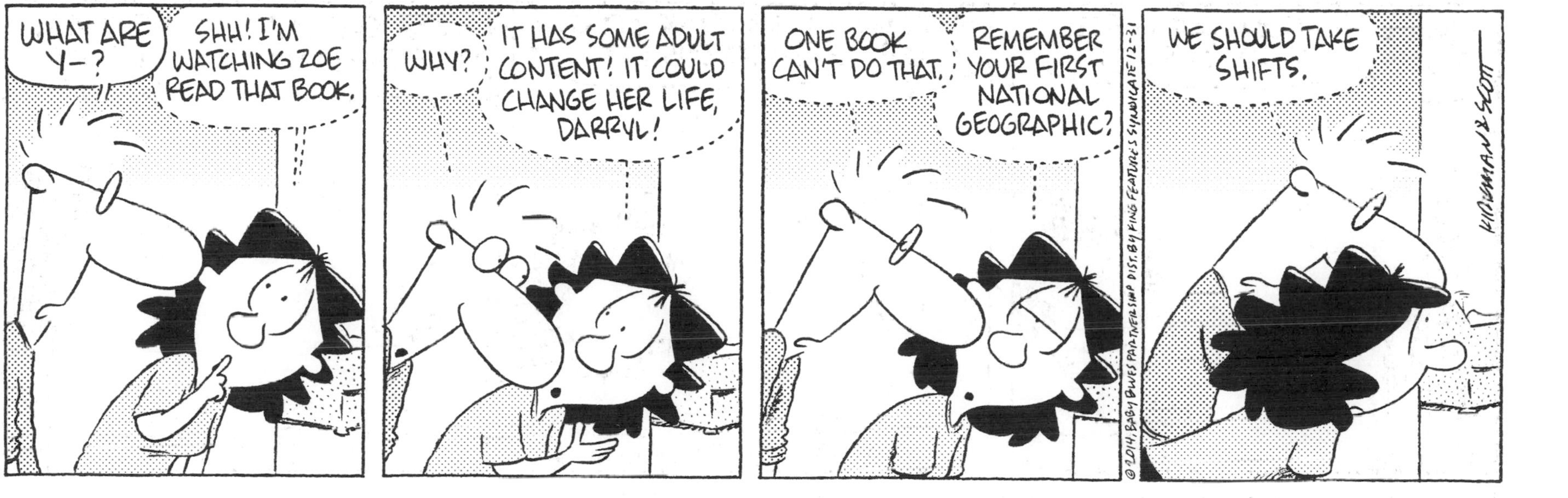
WHAT ARE Y–?
SHH! I'M WATCHING ZOE READ THAT BOOK.
WHY?
IT HAS SOME ADULT CONTENT! IT COULD CHANGE HER LIFE, DARRYL!
ONE BOOK CAN'T DO THAT.
REMEMBER YOUR FIRST NATIONAL GEOGRAPHIC?
©2014, BABY BLUES PARTNERSHIP DIST. BY KING FEATURES SYNDICATE 12-31
WE SHOULD TAKE SHIFTS.
KIRKMAN & SCOTT

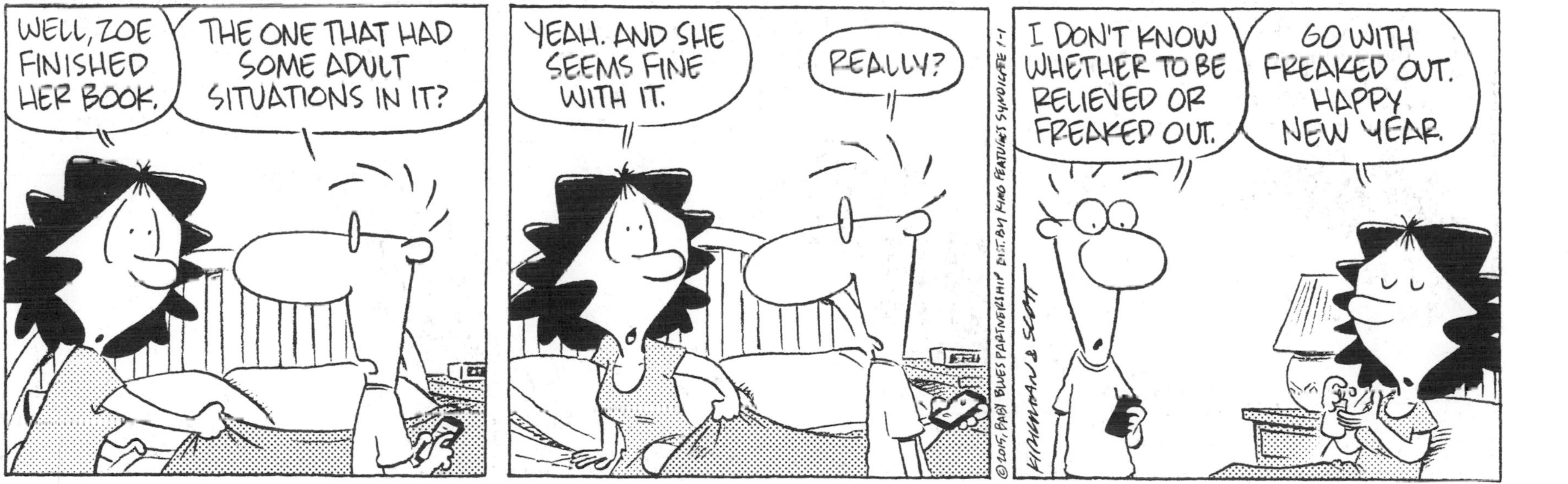
WELL, ZOE FINISHED HER BOOK.
THE ONE THAT HAD SOME ADULT SITUATIONS IN IT?
YEAH. AND SHE SEEMS FINE WITH IT.
REALLY?
©2015, BABY BLUES PARTNERSHIP DIST. BY KING FEATURES SYNDICATE 1-1
KIRKMAN & SCOTT
I DON'T KNOW WHETHER TO BE RELIEVED OR FREAKED OUT.
GO WITH FREAKED OUT. HAPPY NEW YEAR.

Rick: Pure genius from Zoe.

Baby Blues® is syndicated internationally by King Features Syndicate, Inc.
For information, write King Features Syndicate, Inc.,
300 West Fifty-Seventh Street, New York, New York 10019.

Andrews McMeel Publishing, LLC
an Andrews McMeel Universal company
1130 Walnut Street, Kansas City, Missouri 64106
www.andrewsmcmeel.com

15 16 17 18 19 SDB 10 9 8 7 6 5 4 3 2 1

ISBN: 978-1-4494-6303-8

Library of Congress Control Number: 2015937244

Find *Baby Blues*® on the Web at www.babyblues.com.

ATTENTION: SCHOOLS AND BUSINESSES
Andrews McMeel books are available at quantity discounts with bulk purchase for educational,
business, or sales promotional use. For information, please e-mail the Andrews McMeel Publishing
Special Sales Department: specialsales@amuniversal.com.